The GOURMET GATOR Cookbook

Recipes for people
who know their place in the food chain

Written by Lindy Brookhart Stevens
with Kurtis & Christopher Stevens

Cartoons by R.J. Ballard

Great Outdoors Publishing Co.
St. Petersburg, Florida

Published by: Great Outdoors Publishing Co.
                4747 28th Street North
                St. Petersburg, Florida 33714
                (727)525-6609 / www.floridabooks.com

ISBN 0-8200-0810-9

First printing March 2002

Printed in the United States of America

Dedication

To God who, through His love and mercy, gives us physical and spiritual life, and who on the fifth day "... created the great creatures of the sea and every living moving thing with which the water teems." (Genesis 1:20)

To my husband Kurtis and son Christopher, the treasures of my heart, for their love and their ideas for this cookbook, and for their patience in enduring countless experimental recipes, all tested without complaint.

To my parents, Gene and Sally Brookhart, for help in myriad ways, including proofreading and keeping me in printer ink.

To Gerald and Sue Brookhart for sharing great recipes and encouragement.

To Mary and the Taylor family, for amusing anecdotes, eating all that gator, and being faithful friends.

To Patty and the Bogart family, for proofreading, encouragement, and prayers.

To Klidell, who encouraged me to keep working on this cookbook, and who found Great Outdoors Publishing.

And finally, to Jan Allyn and the folks at Great Outdoors Publishing for giving this cookbook a chance.

"... MINDLESS COMPARISONS ASIDE,
NEITHER OF US HAS LIPS ... AND THAT'S A FACT."

Table of Contents

MEATS & MAIN COURSES

GOURMET GATOR DISHES

...the alligators were in such incredible numbers, and so close together from shore to shore, that it would have been easy to have walked across on their heads, had the animals been harmless...

—William Bartram, *Travels*, 1791

Preface

Creating *The Gourmet Gator Cookbook* has been a culinary adventure for me. Sharing that adventure with others is by far the most rewarding aspect of this project.

I hope that this book will not only entertain and educate, but will also inspire and challenge cooks everywhere to expand their cooking horizons to include alligator dishes. For, although these recipes are accompanied by clever cartoons and quirky gator facts, this cookbook is no mere novelty. It is a sincere attempt to introduce the delights of preparing, serving, and eating dishes featuring alligator.

Some may consider writing a cookbook based on cooking alligator an unusual pursuit. But given my cooking background and my conviction that alligator deserves to be a cutting-edge culinary ingredient, it seems entirely logical to me.

I grew up in the kitchens of parents and grandparents who brought meat to the table from farms, fields and forests. They inspired me to be grateful for whatever nature provided. I was also challenged to embrace their attitude that every meat was good to eat if it was cooked well.

An attractive quality of alligator meat is its great versatility. Each cut has its own distinct texture and incomparable flavor. Yet it combines well with other ingredients and lends itself to enhancement with spices, herbs and sauces—providing unparalleled opportunities for variety.

No longer is alligator served only as batter-coated, deep-fried tidbits in Southern restaurants that cater to tourists. More and more frequently one finds menus offering a selection of gator dishes, in restaurants ranging from quaint to elegant.

The Gourmet Gator Cookbook is no exception to this trend. I have included both traditional recipes and "reinvented" gator dishes ranging from starters like soups and salads to more sophisticated and internationally-inspired fare.

Few of the recipes are complicated. A willingness to try new things is more important than any specific cooking skill. Consider these recipes a base from which to start your own adventure in alligator cooking. Keeping textures and flavors in mind, experiment with unusual combinations. Combine gator with fresh ingredients from your region. Customize these recipes and make them your own. You will be rewarded with dishes rich in texture, aroma and variety. The possibilities are limited only by your imagination.

For those with an insurmountable reluctance to eating alligator, alternatives to gator meat are offered in several recipes. You can also substitute appropriate ingredients of your choice, but I would urge you to give alligator a try before dismissing it. I believe you will be pleasantly surprised at just how delicious alligator can be.

Let the adventure begin!

Becoming a Great Gator Chef

Locating sources for alligator meat is the first step in becoming a proficient gator chef. In southern coastal states, legally-obtained, inspected, and documented alligator meat is available from alligator farms, full-service fish markets and butcher shops, and other retailers. Some will ship meat frozen, packed in dry ice. The internet is a good source for finding sellers of processed alligator meat nationwide.

Fresh alligator meat is not widely available, even to those living in southern coastal areas. Gator meat is most commonly sold frozen by the pound in fillets, nuggets, tail meat, and ribs. Occasionally other cuts are available as well. If you do obtain fresh meat and wish to freeze a portion of it, first place it in an airtight container and cover it with water.

When purchasing frozen alligator, ask when it was frozen. Frozen gator meat can have excellent texture and flavor, but as with frozen fish and other meats, quality begins to decline after six months. If stored in relatively airtight packages and at consistently low temperatures, alligator meat is edible for up to a year or longer.

Whether you purchase fresh or frozen alligator meat, it is always helpful to obtain as much information as the retailer is able or willing to provide. For example, knowing if the gator was farm-raised or harvested from the wild in a legal hunt will help you choose which cooking methods and recipes to use.

Because farm-raised alligators are less active than their wild counter-parts and have more consistent diets, their meat is more tender, lighter in color, and milder in flavor. This meat would be acceptable in most recipes, including those with few spices and no sauces. On the other hand, meat from a gator taken in the wild can be tougher and often has an incompa-rable gamey taste that some people prefer. It benefits from longer, slower cooking and is not overpowered by heavy sauces or strong spices.

The age or size of a gator is not always known, but it can also serve as an indicator of flavor. Meat from larger gators—over five feet—is stronger tasting and tougher as a general rule. An alligator between three and five feet generally renders meat that is prime in texture and taste.

Once you obtain the alligator meat, cooking it is a relatively simple process requiring only a bit of seasoning and a few minutes of cooking time. Alligator meat can be prepared in a variety of ways: you can fry it, poach it, bake it, steam it, roast it, sauté it, or grill it. Just be careful not to overcook it.

Choose a method and recipe to suit the available meat and your taste, and begin your culinary adventure.

Alligator Cooking Methods

Cooking alligator may seem daunting at first, but once you've mastered a few simple techniques and familiarized yourself with the various cuts of gator available, you will be surprised at how quickly you will become a "seasoned" gator chef.

Frying   This is the cooking method most widely used by restaurants serving alligator in the southeastern states. Deep frying coated gator bits in hot vegetable oil keeps the meat moist by sealing in the juices. It is suitable for any small bits of gator meat and works well with a variety of coatings from bread crumbs to heavier flour mixtures.

Poaching   Simmering firm-fleshed alligator meat in a liquid flavored with herbs and vegetables produces moist meat with a clam-like flavor. It also provides a rich broth that makes an intriguing base for soups and chowders.

Baking   Special care must be taken not to overcook alligator when baking it. The delicate meat cooks quickly and can become dry. Using a cover while baking and introducing liquids pre-serves the texture of the meat and keeps it moist.

Steaming   Steaming allows the meat to retain its moisture, texture, and unique flavor. It is important not to oversteam the meat if it is to remain tender and not become chewy.

Roasting   You can roast larger cuts of gator, such as whole tails, uncov-ered in a hot oven. The results are similar to cooking a large fish by this method: a papery, crisp exterior and flesh with a concentrated flavor. Stuffing the tail with herbs, citrus slices or vegetables will enhance the flavor of the meat.

Sautéing   Gator fillets can be sautéed successfully with a bit of care. Choose thick, meaty fillets. Coat them with seasoned flour and cook in very hot fat to seal in the juices; then reduce the heat to medium and sauté for 2 to 3 minutes on each side.

Grilling   This cooking method adds rich, smoky flavors to the meat and gives it crispy, brown edges. But not every piece of gator meat is suitable for grilling, Choose a thick, meaty wedge of meat to obtain a good texture, one that is not tough and chewy. Basting with a natural oil is imperative to keep the meat moist.

Suggestions for Safely Handling Alligator Meat

The same precautions that cooks observe when handling other raw meat apply to gator, too. For example:

1 Keep alligator meat frozen until just before you are ready to cook it. Defrost the portion of meat you wish to cook overnight, in the coldest part of your refrigerator. You'll have meat with a firm, moist texture if you defrost it this way. Never thaw it at room temperature. Defrosting alligator in a microwave oven, while safe, is not recommended due to loss of moisture and resulting texture changes.

2 Use plastic or glass cutting boards to cut up raw meat. Clean them thoroughly with hot, soapy water after each use. Until it has been washed, do not use a cutting board that has been used for raw meat to cut other foods that will be consumed raw, such as vegetables for a salad.

3 Wash utensils that have been used with raw gator meat in hot, soapy water before using them with cooked foods.

4 Do not place other foods on the same dishes used for uncooked gator meat until after you have washed them in hot, soapy water.

5 Cook alligator meat thoroughly. Check the meat for doneness by cutting into the thickest part of the meat before serving. The juices from the meat should run clear with no hint of pink or red. A meat thermometer placed in the thickest part of the meat should reveal a temperature of at least 140°F.

6 Place any leftover, cooked gator meat into the refrigerator or freezer within two hours of the time it has finished cooking. This will prevent bacterial growth. Cooked gator meat stored in an airtight container will remain fresh for 2 to 3 days after cooking. It may be frozen for longer storage.

Alligator Cuts Offer Quality and Variety

1. Shoulder steak, shoulder roast

2. Ribs, rib chops, riblets

3. Legs or "wings"

4. Stew meat, ground meat

5. Flank steak, ground meat

6. Round steak, ground meat, nuggets

7. Gator tail fillets, nuggets, cutlets, roasts

8. Tail meat, whole tail, tail bones, fillets, roasts, steaks

Alligator Meat is Delicious and Nutritious

In addition to its versatility and unique flavor, alligator is a nutritionally sound source of protein. It is also low in calories and low in saturated fat. However, it is high in monounsaturated fatty acids, the fats that are believed to raise "good" cholesterol levels.

Additionally, alligator meat is low in sodium and a good source of niacin and vitamin B12, and an excellent source of potassium and phosphorus.

A four-ounce portion of alligator meat is approximately 97% fat free. Fat content varies slightly depending upon whether the animal is farm-raised or wild, due to differences in diet and activity level, but alligator meat seldom exceeds 5% fat. A four-ounce farm-raised fillet contains around 145 calories and 66 milligrams of cholesterol. An equal portion of beef, pork, lamb, or chicken contains more calories and cholesterol.

(Source: Florida Department of Agriculture and Consumer Services)

Appetizers & Snacks

1 BEST PART
2 NEXT TO BEST PART
3 PRETTY GOOD PARTS
4 BETTER THAN NOTHING

Gator Po' Boy

Po' Boy sandwiches can be made with a variety of seafoods, including fried oysters or soft-shelled crabs.

1½ cups unsalted crackers, crushed into crumbs
1½ teaspoons ground red pepper
¾ teaspoon salt
½ teaspoon paprika
⅛ teaspoon garlic powder
2 large eggs, slightly beaten
1 tablespoon milk
1 pound alligator fillet, cut into strips
vegetable oil for deep frying
2 cups shredded lettuce
2 teaspoons sweet onion, minced
2 ripe tomatoes, cut into slices
4 crusty, seeded hoagie rolls, split with centers slightly hollowed
tartar or cocktail sauce (recipes follow)
lemon wedges

1 In a shallow dish, combine cracker crumbs, red pepper, salt, paprika, and garlic powder.

2 In mixing bowl, beat eggs and milk together. Set aside.

3 In Dutch oven or deep-fat fryer, heat oil to 375°F. Dip gator pieces into egg mixture, allowing excess to drip back into bowl. Dredge gator pieces in crumbs.

4 Fry gator strips 3 or 4 at a time; separate them with a spoon as necessary to keep them from sticking together or to the bottom of the pan. When golden, remove with a slotted spoon and drain on paper towels, placing them in oven set on low to keep warm. Repeat until all pieces are cooked.

5 Open rolls and place equal amounts of lettuce on each. Arrange gator strips on top of lettuce. Top with minced onion and tomato slices. Serve immediately with lemon wedges and choice of sauce (see next page).

Yield: 4 sandwiches

Cocktail Sauce

⅓ cup chili sauce
⅓ cup prepared horseradish
1 teaspoon lemon juice

Combine ingredients in a small bowl and mix well until blended.

Yield: ⅔ cup

Tartar Sauce

½ cup mayonnaise
2 tablespoons finely chopped dill pickles
1 tablespoon minced sweet onion
1 tablespoon finely chopped parsley
⅛ teaspoon ground red pepper

Combine ingredients in a small bowl. Mix well; cover and refrigerate 2 hours.

Yield: ⅔ cup

GATOR FACT
The name alligator comes from the Spanish "el lagarto," meaning "the lizard." Just imagine what European explorers in the New World must have thought when they first spied an alligator!

Alligator Canapés

1 1-pound alligator fillet
2 tablespoons butter
4 peppercorns
1 green onion, chopped
4 cloves garlic, peeled and chopped
6 tablespoons mayonnaise
6 tablespoons sour cream
3 tablespoons Old Bay® Seasoning
3 seedless cucumbers
2 tablespoons lemon juice
2 ounces fresh chives, chopped
2 teaspoons paprika

1 Rinse fillet and pat dry with paper towels. Cut fillet into 20 bite-sized pieces.

2 Melt butter in heavy skillet. Add meat and sauté for 3 minutes. Add peppercorns, green onion, and garlic. Sauté, stirring constantly, for 5 to 8 minutes or until meat is lightly browned and onions are soft. Remove from heat and set aside.

3 Combine mayonnaise, sour cream, and Old Bay® Seasoning in mixing bowl.

4 Rinse and dry cucumbers; cut each one into 10 thick slices. Sprinkle each slice with a few drops of lemon juice. Top with a teaspoonful of mayonnaise mixture, a piece of gator meat, and another spoonful of mayonnaise mixture. Sprinkle paprika on top and garnish with chives. Refrigerate to chill and serve cold.

Yield: 20 canapés

Gerald's Gator and Shrimp Hors D'Oeuvres

These tasty treats, created by Gerald and Sue Brookhart, can be cooked on the grill or under the broiler. You may wish to brush these delectable tidbits with barbecue sauce, then cook them for an additional minute on each side.

> 1 1-pound alligator fillet, about 1 inch thick
> 1 pound large raw shrimp, fresh or frozen
> 6 tablespoons prepared white horseradish
> 1 pound center-cut bacon strips
> vegetable oil cooking spray
> 1 cup prepared barbecue sauce (optional)

1 Rinse fillet and pat dry with paper towels. Cut into 1-inch by 3-inch strips. Make shallow slits 1½ inches long down the center of each piece of meat. Set aside.

2 Remove shells from raw shrimp, except for the portion that covers the tail. "Butterfly" each shrimp by making a deep cut down center of the back; remove black sand vein. Rinse shrimp and pat dry. Set aside.

3 Place a half-teaspoon of horseradish into the slit in each piece of gator meat. Place a dollop of horseradish into the center of each shrimp.

4 Wrap a slice of bacon around each shrimp and around each piece of gator tail. Thread each piece of meat or shrimp on a grilling skewer, or secure bacon pieces with wooden toothpicks.

5 Spray grill with cooking spray. Heat grill. Place shrimp and gator bundles on grill for 5 to 8 minutes. Turn and cook for an additional 5 to 8 minutes, or until bacon is crisp and meat is cooked. Serve immediately.

Yield: 8 servings

Fried Gator Fritters

Inspiration for this recipe came from the conch fritters made throughout the Caribbean Islands. Crabmeat also works well in this recipe as a substitute for alligator.

2 teaspoons butter
½ pound boneless alligator meat, finely chopped
1 small onion, minced
1 cup prepared biscuit mix
¼ teaspoon salt
⅛ teaspoon garlic powder
½ teaspoon ground red pepper
1 tablespoon fresh parsley, chopped
½ teaspoon grated lemon peel
¼ cup milk
1 large egg
2 tablespoons fresh lemon juice
¼ teaspoon Worcestershire sauce
vegetable oil for frying
prepared barbecue sauce, sweet and sour sauce, or
    orange marmalade (optional)

"TODAY, I AM RECOMMENDING THE CHICKEN."

1   Melt butter in skillet over medium heat. Add chopped gator and onion and cook, stirring frequently, until meat is browned. Remove mixture from skillet with slotted spoon and place on paper towels to drain. Set aside.

2   In a mixing bowl, stir together biscuit mix, salt, garlic powder, red pepper, parsley, and lemon peel. Press a fist into the center of the mixture to make a well. Set aside.

3   Whisk together milk, egg, lemon juice, and Worcestershire sauce. Pour mixture into well made in dry ingredients. Stir gently, just enough to moisten dry ingredients. Add the gator meat and onion, and stir until well mixed.

4   Fill a heavy skillet 2 inches deep with vegetable oil. Heat oil to 375°F over medium-high heat. Drop batter by spoonfuls into hot oil and fry, a few at a time, for 30 seconds or until golden brown. Remove with slotted spoon and drain on paper towels. Serve immediately with sauce of choice.

Yield: 40 fritters

Layered Alligator Appetizer

12 ounces cream cheese, softened
2 tablespoons mayonnaise
2 tablespoons Worcestershire sauce
1 tablespoon lemon juice
2 cloves garlic, peeled and minced
1 small onion, minced
½ cup water
1 pound alligator fillets
¼ teaspoon salt
½ cup chili sauce
½ teaspoon paprika
2 tablespoons fresh chopped parsley
crackers

1 Combine cream cheese, mayonnaise, Worcestershire sauce, lemon juice, and garlic in a mixing bowl. Using an electric mixer set on medium speed, beat mixture until it is smooth. Stir in chopped onion. Spread mixture to cover the bottom of a shallow dish or pie pan, pushing mixture up around sides of dish to form a small rim. Cover and chill for 3 to 4 hours.

2 In heavy skillet or Dutch oven, combine water and salt. Bring to a boil and add gator meat. Cover, reduce heat, and simmer for 10 to 15 minutes or until meat is done. Drain and chill gator meat.

3 With knife and fork, cut gator meat into thin "sticks" about ⅛ inch wide and 2 inches long.

4 Spread chili sauce over cream cheese mixture and top with gator meat. Garnish with paprika and parsley. Serve with crackers.

Yield: 14 appetizer servings

Marinated Gator Fondue

1½ pounds boneless alligator meat
½ cup low-sodium soy sauce
4 tablespoons water (divided)
2 teaspoons onion, minced
1 clove garlic, peeled and minced
¼ teaspoon dried tarragon
½ cup butter
3 egg yolks
¼ teaspoon salt
peanut oil for frying

1 Rinse gator meat and pat dry with paper towels. Cut meat into 1-inch cubes. Place meat in a shallow dish and add soy sauce, tossing to coat meat. Cover and marinate for 4 hours in refrigerator.

2 In a saucepan, combine 2 tablespoons water, onion, garlic, and tarragon. Bring to a simmer over medium heat and cook for 5 minutes, stirring frequently. Reduce heat to warm and add butter, stirring as it melts.

3 In small mixing bowl, blend egg yolks, 2 tablespoons water and salt. Add to hot mixture and stir until well mixed. Pour dipping sauce into serving dish.

4 Pour peanut oil into fondue pot, filling it about ¾ full. Heat oil to just below the smoking point. At table, guests spear gator cubes on fondue forks and cook them in hot oil for 1 to 2 minutes or to desired doneness. Serve with dipping sauce.

Yield: 4 servings

Reptile Rumaki

4 strips of bacon, cut in half
1 four-ounce alligator fillet, 1½ inches thick, cut into 8 pieces
1½ teaspoons paprika
¼ teaspoon minced fresh ginger
1 green onion, thinly sliced
2 tablespoons lemon juice
minced fresh chives for garnish

1 Partially cook bacon slices (2 minutes in microwave on high). Drain on paper towel and set aside.

2 Sprinkle paprika and ginger on gator bits. Top with green onion. Drizzle each piece of gator with lemon juice as evenly as possible.

3 Wrap a piece of bacon around each piece of gator, securing it with a wooden toothpick.

4 Place meat on a lightly-greased broiler pan and broil for 3 to 4 minutes on each side, until bacon is crisp and gator is done. Drain on paper towels, then garnish and serve warm.

Yield: 8 pieces

GATOR FACT
Florida and Louisiana have the highest populations of alligators in the United States. The largest alligator ever captured in Florida was over 14½ feet long; the heaviest weighed over 1,000 pounds. Louisiana's record gator was bigger yet, at 19 feet, 2 inches. It was collected in 1890.

Kurt's Gator Shish Kabobs

These tasty kabobs also can be made with chunks of tuna or salmon.

> 1 pound alligator fillets
> ½ teaspoon salt
> ¼ teaspoon ground black pepper
> 2 cups olive oil
> 2 cloves garlic, peeled and minced
> 1 tablespoon lemon juice
> ½ teaspoon dried thyme
> ½ teaspoon dried oregano
> ½ teaspoon paprika
> 1 large Bermuda onion, cut into chunks
> 1 green bell pepper, cut into 2-inch chunks
> 2 yellow summer squashes, cut into thick slices
> 8 cherry tomatoes

1 Rinse gator meat and pat dry. Cut meat into 2-inch cubes. Sprinkle with salt and pepper. Set aside.

2 Combine olive oil, garlic, lemon juice, thyme, oregano, and paprika in a mixing bowl. Place gator meat in a shallow dish with cover, or in a plastic bag with zipper top. Pour oil mixture over gator meat and place it in the refrigerator to marinate for 1 to 2 hours, turning occasionally.

3 Remove gator meat from marinade. Thread 8 shish kabob skewers, alternating gator meat cubes, pepper, tomatoes, onion and squash. Place skewers in a shallow dish. Pour remaining marinade over skewers. Cover and refrigerate 1 hour.

4 Heat grill to medium-hot. Place skewers 4 inches from heat source and grill, turning frequently, for 8 to 10 minutes or until meat and vegetables are tender.

Yield: 4 servings of 2 skewers each

Beer Batter Gator Bites

This recipe for beer batter was gleaned from Uncle Gerald Brookhart. When asked by nephew Christopher, then age 6, what he was pouring into the batter, Gerald replied, "It's batter sauce." To which Christopher responded, "It sure looks like a can of beer to me." When heated to at least 160°F, the alcohol burns off, leaving only flavor.

> vegetable oil for frying
> 1 pound alligator fillets, cut into bite-sized pieces
> 1 cup plus 3 tablespoons buttermilk baking mix (divided)
> ½ teaspoon salt
> ⅛ teaspoon ground black pepper
> ¼ teaspoon granulated sugar
> 1 egg
> ½ cup beer

1 Heat oil in a large, heavy skillet or Dutch oven.

2 Lightly coat gator in 3 tablespoons of baking mix. Mix remaining 1 cup baking mix, salt, pepper, sugar, egg, and beer until smooth. Dip fillets into mixture, letting excess drip into bowl.

3 Fry gator pieces until golden brown, about 2 minutes on each side.

Yield: 4 servings

Jerked Gator Strips

1 pound alligator fillets
1½ tablespoons extra virgin olive oil
2 ounces red wine vinegar
3 green onions, minced
1 tablespoon allspice
2 cloves garlic, peeled and minced
1 teaspoon ground coriander
½ teaspoon cinnamon
1 teaspoon granulated sugar
½ teaspoon low-sodium soy sauce
¼ teaspoon ground nutmeg
⅛ teaspoon cayenne pepper

1 Rinse gator meat and pat dry with paper towels. Cut meat into strips approximately 1½ inches by 4 inches. Set aside.

2 Pour olive oil into a mixing bowl. Add remaining ingredients and mix thoroughly.

3 Rub oil and spice mixture evenly on each piece of gator meat. Place in a covered dish in the refrigerator for at least 8 hours or overnight.

4 Preheat broiler. Place gator pieces on broiling pan and broil for 6 to 8 minutes on each side or until cooked through.

Yield: 4 servings

Spicy Gator Balls

1 pound sharp Cheddar cheese
½ pound ground alligator meat (see note below)
½ pound spicy ground sausage
6 drops hot sauce
1 clove garlic, peeled and minced
½ teaspoon salt
¼ teaspoon ground black pepper
½ teaspoon dried onion flakes or onion powder
¼ teaspoon paprika
½ teaspoon dried parsley flakes
2 cups prepared biscuit mix

1 Grate cheese and set it aside to stand at room temperature for 30 minutes.

2 Mix gator meat, sausage, hot sauce, garlic, salt, pepper, onion, paprika, and parsley with biscuit mix. Add cheese and blend until well mixed.

3 Roll mixture into 1-inch balls. Place on an ungreased baking sheet. Bake at 300°F for 20 minutes.

Yield: 15 to 20 gator balls

NOTE: When **ground gator meat** is available, often it is preseasoned. You can also grind your own in a meat grinder or in your food processor. If using a food processor, cut the meat into 1-inch cubes and process the pieces a few at a time, for 10 pulses.

Alligator and Crabmeat Cocktail

Lobster or scallops are delicious substitutions for the crabmeat in this recipe.

    1 6-ounce alligator fillet
    6 ounces crabmeat
    1 6-ounce can Mandarin orange sections, drained
    1 tablespoon lemon juice
    ¼ cup mayonnaise
    ¼ cup plain yogurt
    1 teaspoon catsup
    1 teaspoon prepared horseradish
    ¼ teaspoon salt
    ⅛ teaspoon ground black pepper
    8 Romaine lettuce leaves, rinsed and dried

1 Cut gator meat into bite-sized pieces. Place gator meat and crab in saucepan. Cover with water. Bring to a boil, then reduce heat and simmer for 8 minutes or until meat is done. Remove from pan with slotted spoon and drain on paper towels. Refrigerate meat until thoroughly chilled.

2 Combine mayonnaise, yogurt, catsup, horseradish, lemon juice, salt and pepper in mixing bowl. Blend well.

3 Line four glass cocktail dishes with lettuce leaves. Arrange Mandarin orange slices atop lettuce leaves. Add chilled gator and crabmeat. Generously drizzle cocktail sauce mixture over meat and serve immediately.

Yield: 4 servings

Sally's Wikki Wikki Gatorballs

This recipe was adapted from a recipe used by Christopher's grandmother, Sally Brookhart. She has used different meats to make these meatballs, such as beef, venison and antelope. The meatballs can be made ahead and frozen in a single layer on a jelly roll pan covered with waxed paper. Once frozen, the gator balls can be stored in the freezer in an airtight container for up to three months.

Meatballs:
- ¾ pound ground gator meat (see note page 32)
- ¾ pound lean ground beef
- 1 small onion, finely minced
- 1 clove garlic, peeled and minced
- 1 large egg, slightly beaten
- ½ cup Italian breadcrumbs
- 2 teaspoons salt
- ½ teaspoon ground black pepper
- 2 tablespoons parsley flakes
- 4 tablespoons olive oil

Sauce:
- 3 12-ounce bottles of prepared chili sauce
- ⅛ cup pineapple juice
- 2 teaspoons cornstarch
- 1 16-ounce jar grape jelly
- 4 slices ripe pineapple, cut into chunks

1 Combine ground gator and ground beef in a large mixing bowl. Mix in the onion, garlic, egg, breadcrumbs, salt, pepper and parsley; blend well. Shape into 1½-inch balls and place on a baking sheet

2 Heat olive oil in a heavy skillet over medium-high heat. Using a large spoon, carefully place meatballs into the hot olive oil. Cook meatballs, turning frequently, for 6 to 7 minutes, or until meatballs are cooked through and browned on all sides. If the oil spatters or the meatballs are browning too quickly, reduce the heat. Remove cooked meatballs from the skillet with a slotted spoon and place on paper towels to drain.

"OH YEAH? AND JUST EXACTLY
WHO TOLD YOU THOSE WERE ALLIGATOR SHOES?"

3 Heat chili sauce in a large saucepan over low heat. Add pineapple juice and cornstarch; stir to mix well. Blend in grape jelly, stirring constantly, until heated thoroughly. Spoon in meatballs and stir to ensure meatballs are coated in mixture. Stir in pineapple pieces. Heat thoroughly and serve.

Yield: Approximately 18 meatballs

Find the Gator

Spicy Swamp Wings

You can purchase gator "wings," actually small legs, dressed and tenderized. When choosing legs, smaller ones work best. If they are not pre-tenderized, add meat tenderizer to the legs with the salt and pepper before frying.

    2 pounds small alligator legs (skinless)
    ½ teaspoon salt
    ¼ teaspoon ground black pepper
    ¾ cup all-purpose flour
    2 tablespoons olive oil
    ¼ cup prepared mustard
    ¼ cup (packed) brown sugar
    1 cup prepared barbecue sauce
    6–8 drops hot sauce

1 Rinse gator legs and pat dry. Season each "wing" with salt and pepper; coat with flour. Heat olive oil in a heavy skillet over medium-high heat. Place wings in skillet and fry just until brown, turning frequently. Remove wings from oil with a slotted spoon and drain on paper towels.

2 Combine mustard, brown sugar, barbecue sauce and hot sauce in a shallow baking dish. Place wings in sauce, turning to coat. Cook in 350°F oven for 15 minutes. Turn wings and spoon sauce to cover them. Cook an additional 15 minutes or until wings are tender.

Yield: 8 servings

Zesty Gator Burgers

¾ pound ground alligator meat (see note page 32)
¼ pound lean ground beef
2 eggs
½ cup dry breadcrumbs
1 small onion, finely chopped
1 clove of garlic, peeled and finely minced
¼ cup mayonnaise
1½ teaspoons prepared white horseradish
¼ teaspoon salt
⅛ teaspoon ground black pepper
⅛ teaspoon paprika
2 tablespoons butter
4 Kaiser-style rolls, split
4 lettuce leaves
1 large ripe tomato

1 In large mixing bowl, combine gator meat, ground beef, eggs, bread-crumbs, onion, garlic, mayonnaise, horseradish, salt, pepper and paprika. Mix well. Shape mixture into four patties of equal size.

2 Melt butter in a heavy skillet over medium heat. Place patties in skillet and cook until brown, 5 to 6 minutes on each side, turning once. Serve on rolls with lettuce and tomato.

Yield: 4 servings

Soups & Salads

"HIGH CARD DRAW.
BEST THREE OUTTA FIVE.
LOSER GOES IN THE SOUP."

Cajun Gator Stew

1 tablespoon vegetable oil
1 medium onion, chopped
1 small red bell pepper, chopped
1 small green bell pepper, chopped
2 cloves garlic, peeled and minced
4 firm, ripe tomatoes, peeled and coarsely chopped
1 bay leaf
1½ teaspoon dried thyme
½ teaspoon dried oregano
½ teaspoon Old Bay® Seasoning
¼ teaspoon hot sauce
¼ teaspoon salt
¼ teaspoon ground black pepper
4 cups water
1 pound alligator fillets, cut into one-inch pieces
½ cup uncooked long grain rice
½ pound small fresh shrimp, unpeeled
1 10-ounce package frozen okra, thawed

1 Heat oil in Dutch oven over medium-high heat. Add onion, garlic and peppers. Cook for 3 to 4 minutes or until tender. Add tomatoes, bay leaf, thyme, oregano, Old Bay® Seasoning, hot sauce, salt, pepper, and water. Reduce heat, cover, and simmer for 20 minutes, stirring frequently.

2 Peel and devein shrimp; set aside. Add rice and gator meat to Dutch oven, stirring to mix well. Simmer, covered, for 15 minutes. Add okra and stir well. Cook 5 minutes. Stir in the shrimp and bring mixture to a boil. Remove from heat. Discard bay leaf and serve hot.

Yield: 10 to 12 servings

Gator Ball Soup

Gator meat is so low in fat that these meatballs will not stick together unless the gator is mixed with some other meat. If you do not wish to use sausage, substitute ground beef.

<u>Gator Balls</u>:
1 pound ground alligator meat (see note page 32)
1 pound mildly spicy ground sausage
⅓ cup Italian or spicy breadcrumbs
2 teaspoons salt
¼ teaspoon ground black pepper
¼ teaspoon dried oregano
2 eggs, slightly beaten

<u>Soup Base</u>:
2 tablespoons olive oil
½ cup finely chopped onion
2 cloves garlic, peeled and chopped
2 quarts water
4 cups low-sodium beef broth
1 bay leaf
¼ teaspoon ground coriander
1 8-ounce can tomato sauce
grated Parmesan cheese

1. Heat olive oil in stockpot or Dutch oven and sauté onions and garlic until tender. Add water, beef broth, bay leaf, coriander and tomato sauce. Bring to a boil, stirring frequently.

2. In mixing bowl, combine ground gator, sausage, breadcrumbs, salt, pepper, oregano, and eggs. Mix well. Form into 1-inch balls and drop into boiling broth.

3. Cover, reduce heat and simmer for 30 minutes or until meatballs are done. Remove bay leaf, spoon into bowls, sprinkle with grated Parmesan cheese and serve.

Yield: 6 to 8 servings

Chunky Gator Gumbo

8 quarts water
5–6 pounds alligator tail meat
1 pound smoked ham slice
1 pound firm, ripe tomatoes, diced
2 green bell peppers, chopped
4 celery ribs, chopped
5 bay leaves
1½ tablespoons salt
1½ tablespoons garlic powder
1½ tablespoons onion
3 tablespoons Worchestershire sauce
10–12 drops hot sauce
¾ cup peanut oil
1½ cups all-purpose flour
3 pounds medium-sized fresh shrimp, unpeeled
¼ cup filé powder
1 16-ounce package frozen okra
10–12 cups cooked long grain rice

1 Bring water to a boil in large stockpot. Add gator meat and ham; cook, partially covered, for 40 minutes or until gator meat is done. Remove gator and ham, reserving stock in pot. Chop gator and ham into bite-sized chunks. Set chopped meat aside.

NOW WE'RE COOKIN'!

2 Return broth to a boil. Stir tomatoes, peppers, celery, bay leaves, salt, garlic powder, onions, Worcestershire sauce and hot sauce into broth. Cook, boiling gently, for 30 minutes.

3 Peel and devein shrimp. Set aside.

4 Whisk together oil and flour in a heavy skillet. Cook over medium heat, stirring constantly for about 25 minutes or until roux* is caramel colored. Gradually add roux into broth mix. Add shrimp, gator, ham and okra. Cook for 5 minutes or until shrimp turn pink. Remove bay leaves. Remove from heat. Add filé powder and mix well. Serve over cooked rice.

Yield: 10 quarts

✱ A roux (pronounced "roo") is created by cooking flour in melted butter or oil and is used as a base for many Cajun dishes. The longer the mixture is cooked, the deeper the color of the resulting roux. Stirring constantly and not overheating are important in creating a good roux. It is often said that the secret to a good Cajun dish is in the roux.

Chris and Kurt's Gator Gallejo

1½ pounds fresh collard greens
1 pound thick chunk of alligator tail meat
¼ pound alligator sausage links
2 quarts water
¼ pound bacon
2 cloves garlic, peeled and crushed
1 onion, chopped
½ green pepper, seeded and chopped
2 ripe tomatoes, chopped
½ teaspoon Old Bay® Seasoning
¼ teaspoon paprika
¼ teaspoon ground black pepper
1 teaspoon salt (divided)
1 16-ounce can great northern beans or navy beans
1 16-ounce can garbanzo beans or chickpeas
4 Red Bliss potatoes, peeled and cubed
¾ teaspoon granulated sugar

1 Rinse collard greens until water is clear and greens are free of grit and dirt. Cut away any browned edges or spots on greens. Set aside.

2 Rinse gator tail meat and cut into one-inch cubes. Set aside. Slice gator sausage into ½-inch rounds and set aside.

3 Bring water to boil in a heavy pot or Dutch oven. Place gator meat, gator sausage and bacon in water and return to a boil. Reduce heat to simmer; add garlic, onion, green pepper, tomatoes, Old Bay® Seasoning, paprika, pepper, and ½ teaspoon of salt. Simmer uncovered for 35 to 45 minutes, stirring occasionally, until gator meat is thoroughly cooked.

4 Gradually add the collard greens, great northern or navy beans, garbanzo beans, potatoes, sugar, and remaining ½ teaspoon of salt to the soup. Stir gently and simmer for an additional 30 minutes.

Yield: 2 quarts

Gator and Black-eyed Pea Soup

1½ teaspoons olive oil
8 ounces boneless alligator meat, cut into ½-inch pieces
1 medium onion, diced
3 cloves garlic, peeled and minced
4½ cups water (divided)
½ teaspoon salt
3 peppercorns
1 pound (2 cups) dried black-eyed peas or navy beans
3 cups reduced-sodium beef broth
3 ounces summer sausage, cut into cubes
3 large carrots, cut into chunks
3 stalks of celery, sliced
1 teaspoon dried sage
1 teaspoon dried thyme
¼ teaspoon ground red pepper
¼ teaspoon ground coriander

1 Heat olive oil in skillet over medium heat. Add gator, onion and garlic; sauté, stirring constantly, for 2 minutes. Add ½ cup water, salt, and peppercorns. Cook for an additional 4 minutes, or until gator is done. Remove gator mixture to paper towel-lined plate to drain. Set aside.

2 Boil 4 cups of water in stockpot or large Dutch oven. Add black-eyed peas and boil, uncovered, for 10 minutes.

3 Add beef broth, sausage, carrots, celery, sage, thyme, red pepper, and coriander. Add gator meat and bring soup to a boil. Cover and reduce heat; simmer for 45 minutes, stirring occasionally.

Yield: 2 quarts

Wild Game and Gator Gumbo

2 quarts water

2½–3 pounds alligator meat (tail or other meat is acceptable)

2 teaspoons salt

8 dove breasts (or 1 pound other game bird)

1 1-pound venison roast, cut into bite-sized cubes

1 rabbit, dressed and quartered

1 squirrel, dressed and cut into bite-sized pieces (optional)

1½ pounds link sausage

1 cup chopped onion (divided)

1 cup chopped celery

3 cloves garlic, minced

1 bay leaf

1 tablespoon salt

½ teaspoon ground black pepper

½ teaspoon red pepper (divided)

¼ cup bacon drippings

½ cup all-purpose flour

1 teaspoon Worcestershire sauce

1 teaspoon hot sauce

12 cups (or more) of hot cooked rice

1 Bring water to a boil in stockpot or large Dutch oven. Add gator meat and 2 teaspoons of salt. Return to boil. Cover, reduce heat, and simmer one hour or until tender. Remove gator from broth and cut into bite-sized pieces Set aside. Keep broth.

2 In Dutch oven or stockpot, combine the dove breasts, venison, squirrel, rabbit, ¼ teaspoon red pepper, 1 tablespoon salt, bay leaf, garlic, and ⅛ cup chopped onion. Cover with water. Bring to a boil; cover, reduce heat and simmer 2 hours.

3 Remove meat from broth. Strain broth and set aside. Remove meat from bones and cut into bite-sized pieces. Set aside.

4 Brown sausage in a heavy skillet over medium heat; remove and drain on paper towels. Add bacon drippings to sausage drippings in skillet.

Heat over medium heat. Add flour and cook, stirring constantly, for 15 minutes or until mixture is a rich caramel color. Add remaining onion, celery and ¼ teaspoon red pepper. Cook an additional 10 minutes.

5 Combine drippings mixture and gator broth in large stockpot or Dutch oven. Cover and simmer 30 minutes. Add gator, dove, venison, rabbit, squirrel, sausage, hot sauce, and Worcestershire sauce. Add game stock if additional liquid is needed. Simmer uncovered for 2 hours, stirring occasionally. (It is important not to overcook the game. Check it frequently for doneness, reducing heat or cooking time if necessary.) Serve hot over cooked rice.

Yield: 12 servings

Gator Tail Soup

1 tablespoon olive oil
3 tablespoons butter
2 pounds alligator tail, cut into 1-inch sections
1 sweet onion, thinly sliced
1 carrot, thinly sliced
2 cloves garlic, peeled and minced
2 tablespoons all-purpose flour
2 quarts beef broth, fresh or prepared low-sodium
1 teaspoon dried thyme
5 peppercorns
1 tablespoon fresh parsley, minced
⅛ teaspoon ground coriander
1 teaspoon salt
1 cup chopped red potatoes
1 cup chopped carrots
2 stalks celery, thinly sliced

1 In Dutch oven or heavy stockpot, heat olive oil and 1 tablespoon butter over medium heat. Add gator tail and cook, turning frequently, until gator tail is browned. Remove gator with slotted spoon and set aside on paper towel to drain. Cook onion, garlic, and sliced carrot in oil for 8 minutes or until lightly browned and soft. Add flour and brown, stirring constantly. Remove pan from heat.

2 Whisk in beef stock and return to heat. Bring to a boil and cook, continuing constant stirring, until sauce is smooth and bubbly. Return gator tail to pot and add thyme, peppercorns, parsley, coriander and salt. Bring to a boil. Reduce heat and simmer, partially covered, for 2½ hours.

3 In skillet, melt 2 tablespoons of butter. Put potatoes, carrots and celery into the butter and cook, stirring frequently for 3 minutes. Add to soup and simmer an additional 30 minutes.

Yield: 4 servings

Savory Gator Soup

1 tablespoon olive oil
1 medium onion, chopped
2 ribs of celery, chopped
1 large carrot, chopped
1 pound alligator meat, cut into bite-sized pieces
¼ cup evaporated milk
3 cups low-sodium beef broth
1 teaspoon ground coriander
1 teaspoon dried sage
1 teaspoon dried oregano
1 bay leaf
1 teaspoon salt
½ teaspoon ground black pepper
1 10-ounce package frozen green peas

1 In stockpot or Dutch oven, heat olive oil over medium heat. Place onion, celery, carrot and gator pieces in pan and cook over medium heat for five minutes or until onion is soft and gator bites are browned.

2 Add broth and simmer for 10 minutes. Add coriander, sage, oregano, bay leaf, salt, pepper and peas. Bring to a boil. Reduce heat and simmer for 8 minutes. Add evaporated milk and simmer until heated, about 2 minutes. Remove bay leaf and serve immediately.

Yield: 4 servings

GATOR FACT
The muscles an alligator uses to open its jaws are very weak; a loop of rope or a piece of duct tape are sufficient to hold its jaws closed. The muscles that close the jaw are extremely strong, however, exerting up to 3,000 pounds per square inch.

Juicy Gator Jambalaya

¼ pound thick-sliced bacon, cut into 1-inch pieces
¼ cup butter
1 large Bermuda onion, chopped
4 cloves garlic, peeled and chopped
1 green bell pepper, cut into strips
1 red bell pepper, cut into strips
1 cup uncooked long grain rice
½ teaspoon dried thyme
1 teaspoon salt
½ teaspoon ground black pepper
1 teaspoon hot sauce
1 bay leaf
2 cups low-sodium chicken stock
½ pound smoked, cooked ham, diced
6 medium-sized firm, ripe tomatoes, diced
1 pound medium-sized raw shrimp, shelled and deveined
1 pound boneless alligator tail meat, diced into cubes
1 tablespoon chopped fresh parsley

1 Preheat oven to 350°F. Place bacon on a microwave-safe plate covered with paper towels and cook in microwave until bacon is brown, but not crisp. Drain bacon on paper towels and set aside.

2 Melt butter over medium heat in heavy ovenproof skillet or Dutch oven; add onion, peppers, gator meat and garlic. Cook until onion is tender, but not brown. Add rice to skillet and cook an additional 3 minutes, stirring constantly. Stir in the bacon, thyme, salt, pepper, hot sauce and bay leaf. Add 2 cups of chicken broth and bring to a boil. Stir in the ham and the tomatoes. Cover and cook for 10 minutes. Add the shrimp and stir well. Place covered Dutch oven or skillet in oven and bake for 10 minutes longer or until rice is cooked. Remove bay leaf, garnish with fresh parsley, and serve.

Yield: 4 to 6 servings

Alligator and Avocado Salad

Avocados that are ripe will yield to a gentle press with your thumb. If an avocado proves too firm, place it in a paper bag and let it ripen for a day or two.

Salad:
1 one-pound alligator fillet
1 tablespoon white or cider vinegar
1 bay leaf
⅛ teaspoon salt
⅛ teaspoon paprika
6 peppercorns
2 cloves garlic, peeled and crushed
half a small cucumber, seeded and chopped
1 3-ounce can sliced black olives
3 medium tomatoes, skinned and sliced
1 leek, minced
1 ripe avocado

Dressing:
3 tablespoons extra-virgin olive oil
2 tablespoons lime juice
1 teaspoon prepared Dijon mustard
1 tablespoon chopped parsley
salt and pepper to taste

1 Rinse fillet, pat dry, and cut into thin strips. Place gator strips in pan with vinegar, bay leaf, salt, paprika, peppercorns, and garlic. Cover with water. Bring to a boil, then cover and reduce heat to simmer. Cook gently for 12 to 15 minutes or until gator is tender. Remove meat carefully with a slotted spoon and set aside to cool.

2 Mix together cooled gator, cucumber, tomatoes, leek, and black olives.

3 Peel and pit the avocado. Chop avocado and add to the gator mixture.

4 Mix dressing ingredients well. Pour over salad and toss lightly. Serve immediately.

Yield: 4 servings

Pineapple Gator Salad

1½ pounds boneless alligator meat
1½ teaspoons olive oil
2 tablespoons water
1 20-ounce can pineapple chunks
1 large cucumber, thinly sliced
1 green onion, thinly sliced, including green top
1 teaspoon salt
½ teaspoon ground black pepper
¼ teaspoon garlic powder
½ teaspoon dried dill
¼ cup sour cream
4 maraschino cherries, halved

1 Rinse gator meat and dry with paper towel. Cut into 1-inch cubes. Heat olive oil in skillet. Add gator meat and cook for 3 to 5 minutes or until lightly browned, turning frequently. Add water and continue cooking for another 3 to 5 minutes or until meat is done. Remove gator with slotted spoon to drain on paper towels. Set aside to cool.

2 Drain pineapple. Place drained pineapple in a large salad bowl; add cucumber slices, onion, and seasonings. Add sour cream and cooled gator meat. Toss to mix, making sure gator is coated with sour cream. Garnish salad with maraschino cherry halves, cover and refrigerate for at least one hour. Serve chilled.

Yield: 6 servings

Find the Gator

Gator and Shrimp Pasta Salad

½ cup medium-sized shrimp, fresh or frozen

2 cups small, tri-colored pasta twists

3 tablespoons extra-virgin olive oil (divided)

⅔ pound boneless alligator meat, cut into bite-sized chunks

1 small onion, finely chopped

¼ cup water

3 green onions, sliced diagonally

1 cup medium mushrooms, sliced

3 small zucchini, sliced

3 small yellow summer squash, sliced

2 teaspoons low-sodium soy sauce

2 tablespoons white wine vinegar

1 teaspoon paprika

1 teaspoon salt

¼ teaspoon ground black pepper

1 Thaw shrimp, if frozen. Cook pasta, following package directions; drain and rinse under cold running water and set aside.

2 In skillet with lid, heat 1 tablespoon olive oil over medium-high heat. Add gator meat and onion. Sauté for 5 minutes or until onions are translucent. Carefully pour in water. Add shrimp, green onions, mushrooms, zucchini, and squash. Cook, stirring frequently, for an additional 2 minutes. Reduce heat, cover and simmer for 5 minutes. Remove from heat.

3 Mix remaining olive oil, soy sauce, vinegar, paprika, salt and pepper. Place cooked pasta in large mixing or salad bowl. Add meat and vegetables to pasta. Spoon olive oil mixture over meat. Gently toss to mix. Cover and chill in refrigerator. Serve cold.

Yield: 4 servings

Southern Collard Greens and Gator Salad

¾ pound alligator meat
6 peppercorns
¼ teaspoon garlic salt
¼ teaspoon paprika
3 tablespoons extra-virgin olive oil (divided)
1 large, sweet onion, diced
1 large red pepper, sliced into ¼-inch wide strips
2 pounds collard greens
¼ cup white vinegar
1 tablespoon sugar
½ teaspoon salt

1 Rinse gator and pat dry; cut into thin, 1-inch by 3-inch strips. Place gator strips in a pan and cover with water. Add peppercorns, garlic salt, and paprika. Bring to a boil. Reduce to simmer and cook for 5 to 7 minutes or until juices run clear. Remove from water with slotted spoon. Set aside to cool.

2 In Dutch oven or large saucepan, heat 2 tablespoons olive oil on medium-high heat. Cook onion, stirring occasionally for 3 minutes, until almost tender. Add red pepper and cook until peppers are tender, but still crisp. Remove to a bowl lined with a paper towel to drain.

3 Rinse collard greens under cool water. Cut off and throw away ribs and stems. Cut leaves into pieces about 2 inches wide Add 1 tablespoon olive oil to Dutch oven and reheat over medium-high heat. Add collards to oil and cook 5 to 8 minutes, stirring constantly. Return gator and pepper mixture to Dutch oven; stir in vinegar, sugar and salt until blended. Cook until heated through. Serve immediately or cover and refrigerate.

Yield: 4 servings

Creamy Gator Salad with Rice

1 pound alligator fillets

½ teaspoon salt

¼ teaspoon paprika

3 tablespoons water

3 peppercorns

1 bay leaf

1 10-ounce package frozen green peas, thawed

1 10-ounce package brown and wild rice mix*, cooked according to package directions

2 ounces Swiss cheese, cut into cubes

2 ounces sharp Cheddar cheese, cut into cubes

2 green onions with tops, chopped diagonally

¼ teaspoon dried dill

2 cups fresh spinach leaves

½ cup shredded carrot

1 plum tomato, diced

1 8-ounce bottle creamy cucumber salad dressing

1 Rinse gator fillets and pat dry. Cut fillets into bite-sized pieces; sprinkle with salt and paprika. In a skillet with a lid, heat water over medium-high heat. Add peppercorns and bay leaf. Bring water to a boil. Add gator meat, cover and steam for 6 to 8 minutes, stirring occasionally, until gator meat is cooked through. Remove meat from skillet with a slotted spoon and set aside on paper towels to drain and cool.

GATOR FACT

The temperature of an alligator's nest determines the gender of the offspring. Cooler temperatures produce more females, while warmer temperatures produce more males. Just the opposite is true with crocodiles.

2 Place thawed peas, rice, cheeses, green onions and gator meat in a salad or mixing bowl. Sprinkle with dill. Toss to mix thoroughly; cover and refrigerate to chill.

3 Rinse and dry spinach leaves. Arrange spinach in the bottom of a shallow salad bowl. Spoon gator mixture on top of spinach, diced tomato on top of gator. Drizzle generously with cucumber dressing, garnish with shredded carrot, and serve.

Yield: 4 to 6 servings

✱ Plain brown rice may be substituted; prepare rice per package directions, but substitute ¾ cup chicken broth for ¾ cup of the water, and along with the uncooked rice add a teaspoon of salt, ½ teaspoon ground black pepper, 1 teaspoon dried sage, ⅔ teaspoon garlic powder and ½ teaspoon onion powder.

Spiced Gator and Okra Salad

¾ pound alligator fillet, cut into strips
2 cups small okra, fresh or frozen
1 cup sweet corn kernels
1 cup chopped tomatoes
1 teaspoon granulated sugar
2 tablespoons lemon juice
1 tablespoon chili sauce
2 cloves garlic, peeled and crushed
2 teaspoons olive oil
1 small, sweet onion, minced
1 teaspoon paprika
1 teaspoon ground coriander
¼ teaspoon ground ginger
¼ teaspoon ground black pepper

1 Boil water in a saucepan. Add gator strips and boil for 5 minutes. Add okra and cook an additional 2 to 3 minutes until okra is tender, but still crisp. Drain and rinse with cool water. Place in a serving bowl.

2 Add corn, tomatoes, sugar, lemon juice, chili sauce, garlic, oil, onion, paprika, coriander, ginger, and pepper. Mix well and cover. Refrigerate at least one hour before serving.

Yield: 4 servings

Meats & Main Courses

"WE'VE BEEN RECEIVING RECONNAISSANCE REPORTS FROM AS FAR AWAY AS THE TIP OF OKLAHOMA; AND, I'M SORRY TO SAY, THE NUMBER OF HUMANS IS MUCH GREATER THAN ORIGINALLY ANTICIPATED — SHOOT! THERE ARE AT LEAST A BAZILLION PEOPLE IN THIS STATE ALONE... F COURSE, ON THE UP SIDE, WE COULD EAT ONE OR TWO, APIECE, PER DAY, AND PROBABLY NEVER RUN OUT."

Alligator Lasagna

2½–3 pounds alligator meat
6 cups water
2 tablespoons butter, melted
1 teaspoon salt
2 cloves garlic, peeled and minced
1 small, sweet onion, minced
4 cups tomato sauce
½ teaspoon dried oregano
¼ teaspoon ground black pepper
1 bay leaf
1 tablespoon granulated sugar
2 cups ricotta cheese
2 cups shredded mozzarella cheese (divided)
2 tablespoons grated Parmesan cheese
8 lasagna noodles, uncooked

1 Place gator in stockpot or Dutch oven. Cover with water and add salt; bring to a boil. Cover, reduce heat and simmer for 30 to 40 minutes or until tender. Drain, reserving the broth. Cool gator slightly. Cut into bite-sized pieces and set aside.

2 Heat butter in Dutch oven and cook onions and garlic in butter for 2 minutes over medium-high heat, stirring constantly. Add tomato sauce, oregano, pepper, bay leaf and sugar. Reduce heat and simmer for 10 minutes, stirring occasionally.

GATOR FACT

Other than humans, adult wild alligators have no natural predators. Hatchlings, however, are preyed upon by fish, fowl, reptile, mammals, and other alligators. Many adults also die from cannibalism, or from injuries sustained while fighting with other alligators.

3 In large pot, bring reserved broth to a boil, adding water if necessary. Cook lasagna noodles according to package directions; drain.

4 In mixing bowl, blend ricotta and Parmesan mozzarella cheeses with half of the mozzarella cheese, reserving the rest for later use. Set cheese mixture aside.

5 Lightly grease a shallow 11-inch by 9-inch baking or casserole dish. Cover the bottom of the dish with a small amount of sauce. Layer with half of the lasagna noodles, gator meat, sauce and cheese mixture Repeat layering with noodles, gator and sauce.

6 Bake at 350°F for 20 minutes; top with reserved mozzarella cheese and bake an additional 7 minutes. Let stand 10 minutes before serving.

Yield: 6 servings

Alligator Pie

¾ pound ground alligator meat (see note page 32)
½ pound lean ground beef
2 cloves garlic, peeled and chopped
1 small onion, chopped
1 small green bell pepper, chopped
½ cup fresh mushrooms, sliced
1 deep-dish pie shell, pre-baked*
2 plum tomatoes, sliced
1 8-ounce can Italian-style tomato sauce
1 teaspoon granulated sugar
1 teaspoon salt
½ teaspoon ground black pepper
½ cup grated Parmesan cheese
1½ cups grated mozzarella cheese

1 Preheat oven to 375°F. In heavy skillet or Dutch oven, combine gator meat and ground beef. Over medium-high heat, brown meat for 3 minutes. Add garlic, onion, bell pepper and mushrooms. Continue cooking, turning frequently, for 5 minutes or until meat is cooked and onions are soft. Remove meat and vegetables from skillet with a slotted spoon. Drain on paper towels and set aside.

2 Place slices from one tomato in a single layer in the bottom of frozen pie shell crust. In mixing bowl, combine meat and vegetable mixture, tomato sauce, sugar, salt and pepper. Spread layer of meat mixture over tomato slices in pie shell. Combine mozzarella and Parmesan cheeses. Put one half of cheese mixture over meat in pie shell. Place remaining tomato slices in single layer over cheese. Pour the meat mixture over tomatoes and top with the rest of the cheese.

3 Bake pie for 15 to 20 minutes. Serve hot.

Yield: 6 servings

✱ If your grocery doesn't carry pre-baked deep-dish pie crusts, you can make your own, as I often do. Press homemade or prepared pie dough

ALLIGATOR PI

into a deep-dish pie pan with your fingertips. Then line the dough with two layers of heavy-duty aluminum foil and bake it in a 450°F oven for 8 minutes. Remove the foil covering and return the crust to the oven for 5 more minutes to brown slightly. Cool on a wire rack.

Alligator Seafood Surprise

3 tablespoons olive oil

½ pound alligator fillet, one inch thick

1 cup celery, chopped

½ cup sweet onion, chopped

½ red or yellow bell pepper, chopped

3 cloves garlic, peeled and crushed

½ pound scallops

½ pound medium shrimp, peeled and deveined

1 cup mayonnaise

½ teaspoon Worcestershire sauce

1 teaspoon lemon juice

½ teaspoon salt

¼ teaspoon ground black pepper

1 cup crushed potato chips

½ teaspoon paprika

¼ cup fresh chopped parsley (or 1 tablespoon dried parsley flakes)

1 Heat olive oil in a heavy skillet. Cut gator fillet into bite-sized pieces. Place gator, onions, celery, peppers and garlic into oil and cook, stirring frequently for 2 minutes. Add scallops and shrimp. Cook an additional 3 to 5 minutes until onions are soft and meat is lightly browned. Removed cooked items from skillet with a slotted spoon and place on a dish covered with paper towels to drain. Set aside.

2 In a large mixing bowl, combine mayonnaise, Worcestershire sauce, lemon juice, salt and pepper. Add meat and vegetables and mix well. Place meat and vegetable mixture in a greased casserole. Cover with crushed potato chips. Bake at 350°F for 30 minutes. Sprinkle with paprika and parsley.

Yield: 6 servings

Cheesy Croc Pasta

¾ pound boneless alligator meat
2 tablespoons olive oil
1 tablespoon butter
2 cloves garlic, minced
3 tablespoons green onion
4 stalks thinly-sliced celery
1 small red pepper, cut into strips
3 tablespoons all-purpose flour
½ teaspoon ground black pepper
2 tablespoons low-sodium soy sauce
2 cups milk or light cream
2 cups sharp Cheddar cheese, shredded
2 cups cooked broccoli florets
¼ cup cooked, sliced mushrooms
⅓ cup water chestnuts
8 ounces linguini, cooked per package directions

1 Rinse gator meat and pat dry. Cut into ½-inch strips and set aside. Heat oil and butter over medium heat in heavy skillet or saucepan. Add gator, garlic, onion, celery and pepper to oil mixture and sauté until gator is done and onions are soft.

2 In mixing bowl, combine flour, pepper and soy sauce. Add to gator mixture and stir to mix well. Gradually add milk, stirring to keep smooth. Bring mixture to a boil and stir constantly for one minute. Reduce the heat to simmer. Stir in the cheese and blend as cheese melts. Stir in broccoli, mushrooms and water chestnuts and heat until warm. Serve over cooked linguini.

Yield: 4 servings

Christopher's Croc Pot Chili

As the title indicates, this dish can be prepared in a crock-pot or slow cooker. If you opt to use a crock-pot, brown the meat and drain it. Put meat and other ingredients into the crock-pot. Stir; add spices and stir again. Cook on low heat for 3 hours or on high for 1½ hours.

1 pound ground alligator meat (see note page 32)
1 pound ground beef
2 onions
1 green bell pepper
4 cloves garlic, peeled and crushed
½ cup fresh mushrooms, sliced
2 16-ounce cans whole stewed tomatoes with juice
1 teaspoon dried oregano
1 teaspoon ground black pepper
1 tablespoon salt
2 teaspoons chili powder
2 teaspoons–2 tablespoons hot sauce, to taste
2 16-ounce cans spicy chili beans
2 tablespoons smooth peanut butter
1 cup shredded Cheddar cheese

1 Mix ground gator meat and ground beef together. Place in large, heavy skillet or Dutch oven. Add onions, pepper, garlic and mushrooms. Cook on medium-high heat, stirring frequently, for 8 to 10 minutes, or until meat is thoroughly cooked. Remove meat and vegetables with a wooden spoon and drain. Set aside. Discard any fat in pan.

2 Pour tomatoes with juice into Dutch oven or stockpot. Add sugar, oregano, pepper, salt, chili powder, and hot sauce. Stir to mix. Bring to a boil. Reduce heat, cover, and simmer 5 minutes. Stir in meat and vegetables. Add beans. Simmer an additional 12 to 15 minutes. Blend in peanut butter and heat throughout. Remove from heat, top with shredded cheese and serve.

Yield: 6 to 8 servings

Find
the
Gator

Gator Tail and Chips

Chips:

vegetable oil for frying

2 pounds russet potatoes, sliced into ¼-inch rounds

Batter:

1 cup all-purpose flour

1 egg yolk

2 tablespoons beer

¼ teaspoon salt

3 tablespoons milk combined with 3 tablespoons cold water

1 egg white

"IF HE TRIES TO TRUMP SOMETHING
OUT OF TURN ... JUST LET HIM HAVE IT."

Gator Tail:
2 pounds firm alligator tail or other fillets, 1–2 inches thick
malt vinegar
salt to taste

1 To cook chips, heat 4 to 5 inches of oil in deep skillet or Dutch oven. Preheat oven to 250°F. Line a jellyroll pan or shallow roasting pan with paper towels.

2 Dry potatoes with a paper towel. Place a handful of potato rounds into the hot oil and deep fry, keeping them turned and separated to avoid burning and sticking. When they are crisp and light brown, use a slotted spoon to place them onto the lined pan to drain, and place them in the oven to keep warm.

3 Make a "hill" of the flour in a large mixing bowl. Press your fist into the center of the flour to make a well. Place the egg yolk, beer, and salt into this indentation. Stir the ingredients together to mix well. Gradually add the milk and water, continuing to stir, until you have a smooth batter.

4 Wash gator under cold running water and pat dry with paper towels. Cut gator fillets into 3-inch by 5-inch pieces.

5 Reheat the 4 to 5 inches of oil (used to cook the chips) in the deep skillet or Dutch oven.

6 Dip each piece of gator into the batter. When it is well coated, carefully place it into the hot oil. Fry 2 or 3 pieces at a time, cooking for 4 or 5 minutes or until golden brown, turning occasionally to prevent sticking.

7 Serve the gator and chips together while gator is still hot. Sprinkle with salt and vinegar to taste.

Yield: 4 servings

Grilled Citrus Gator

6 tablespoons lemon juice
4 tablespoons lime juice
2 cloves garlic, peeled and crushed
2 teaspoons paprika
½ teaspoon salt
¼ teaspoon ground black pepper
1 tablespoon butter, melted
½ cup honey-Dijon mustard salad dressing
4 alligator fillets, about 6 ounces each
1 lemon, sliced into thin rounds (garnish)
1 lime, sliced into thin rounds (garnish)

1 Combine lemon juice, lime juice, garlic, paprika, salt, pepper, butter and salad dressing in a covered bowl or zippered plastic bag.

2 Place gator fillets in bag or bowl with marinade; let stand in refrigerator for a minimum of 30 minutes, turning at least once to ensure even marinating.

3 Remove gator from marinade and grill over medium heat for 5 minutes on each side or until done.

4 Arrange gator fillets on serving dish; garnish with alternating slices of lemon and lime.

Yield: 4 servings

Sweet Glazed Gator Ribs

Gator ribs contain less fat and are more delicate than traditional beef or pork ribs. Keeping the ribs marinated and taking special care not to over-cook them will result in juicier and more flavorful ribs.

- 5 pounds alligator ribs, uncut
- 1¾ teaspoons salt
- 1¼ teaspoons ground black pepper
- 4 tablespoons butter
- 1 medium onion, chopped
- 4 cloves garlic, chopped
- ¾ teaspoon Worcestershire sauce
- 6 dashes mild red pepper sauce
- 4 teaspoons brown sugar, packed
- ½ teaspoon dry mustard
- ½ cup honey
- 1 teaspoon low sodium soy sauce

1 Preheat oven to 350°F. Wash ribs and pat dry. Sprinkle with salt and pepper. Wrap in heavy-duty aluminum foil. Place in a roasting pan and bake for 1 hour.

2 Make sauce by melting butter over medium heat in a saucepan. Sauté onion in butter for 4 minutes. Add garlic and sauté for 1 minute. Stir in remaining ingredients; boil for 1 minute. Reduce heat and simmer for 5 minutes.

3 Drain ribs. Place ribs on grill and baste with sauce. Grill 6 to 9 minutes. Turn and baste other side with sauce. Grill an additional 10 minutes or until done.

4 Reheat remaining sauce just to boiling. Cut ribs apart, brush them with sauce, and serve.

Yield: 6 to 8 servings

Perlieu Gator Stew

Perlieu can be made with a variety of meats, including squirrel, venison, or chicken. It is a derivative of Turkish pilaf, and contains rice and meat in a seasoned broth.

2 pounds boneless alligator tail meat
2 tablespoons vegetable oil
1 16-ounce can chicken broth
½ pound Red Bliss potatoes
½ pound Yukon Gold or white potatoes
1 fresh parsnip, peeled and cubed (optional)
2 large onions, peeled and quartered
1 bay leaf
1 tablespoon Old Bay® Seasoning
1 tablespoon salt
2 teaspoons flaked red pepper
1 16-ounce can cream-style white corn
6 firm, ripe tomatoes, quartered
½ cup cooked rice
¼ pound butter
2 tablespoons fresh parsley, minced

1 Rinse gator meat under running water. Pat dry. Cut gator meat into 1-inch cubes and set aside.

2 Heat vegetable oil in heavy skillet. Cook gator meat in oil for 3 to 5 minutes, turning to brown it on all sides. Remove meat from skillet with a slotted spoon and drain on paper towels.

3 Pour broth into Dutch oven or stockpot. Bring to a gentle boil over medium-high heat.

4 Rinse red and gold potatoes and cut them into 2-inch chunks, leaving skins intact. Add potatoes, parsnips, onions, bay leaf, Old Bay® Seasoning, salt, and red pepper to broth. Reduce heat and simmer, uncovered, for 20 minutes.

"HON - THE BATHROOM DOOR IS STUCK."

"YEAH, IT DOES THAT SOMETIMES WHEN THE WINDOW IS LEFT OPEN . . . SEEMS TO RELEASE ON ITS OWN THOUGH, IF YOU LEAVE IT ALONE LONG ENOUGH."

5 Stir gator meat into broth and vegetable mixture. Add corn, tomatoes, rice and butter. Cook for an additional 45 minutes, stirring occasionally to prevent sticking. Sprinkle parsley over stew and serve.

Yield: 6 servings

Crispy Gator Cutlets

4 alligator fillets, 6–8 ounces each
1 egg white
¼ teaspoon water
1 cup finely chopped pecans
4 tablespoons all-purpose flour
½ teaspoon salt
¼ teaspoon ground black pepper
¼ teaspoon paprika
1 tablespoon butter or margarine
1 tablespoon vegetable oil

1 Flatten gator fillets to ¼-inch thickness. In a shallow pan or bowl, beat the egg white with ¼ teaspoon water. In a second shallow pan or bowl, combine the pecans, flour, salt, pepper and paprika.

2 Dip the gator fillets one at a time in the egg white, then coat with pecan mixture.

3 In a large, heavy skillet, heat oil and butter on medium heat. Add the gator fillets and cook for 3 to 5 minutes on each side until done.*

Yield: 4 servings

✱ If you use this recipe for gator filets that are more than 1½ inches thick, or substitute poultry or another meat, increase the cooking time until juices run clear.

GATOR FACT

Unless they've been fed, wild alligators generally are sluggish and avoid people. However, they can become aggressive if disturbed or annoyed, and may lunge after a perceived threat, reaching a speed of up to 11 mph. Never, ever, feed a wild alligator, and keep your distance—stay at least 25 yards away.

Mississippi Grilled Gator

2 pounds alligator fillets, about 1½ inches thick
¼ pound (1 stick) butter
1 small, sweet onion, minced
2 cloves garlic, peeled and minced
1 cup tomato sauce
¼ teaspoon dried oregano
¼ teaspoon paprika
¼ teaspoon salt
⅛ teaspoon ground black pepper
2 tablespoons brown sugar, firmly packed
1 teaspoon hot red pepper
1 tablespoon lemon juice

1 Heat grill. Place grilling rack 5 to 6 inches above source of heat.

2 Melt butter in a small saucepan over medium heat. Add onion and garlic and cook, stirring occasionally, for 3 minutes or until soft.

3 Add tomato sauce, oregano, paprika, salt, pepper, brown sugar, red pepper, and lemon juice. Stirring constantly, bring mixture to a simmer. Remove sauce from heat when sugar has completely dissolved.

4 Place gator fillets on grill and baste with sauce. Cook 6 to 9 minutes on each side, turning once and basting occasionally.

Yield: 5 to 6 servings

Saurian Steak Supreme

1 pound alligator tail steaks
½ cup extra-virgin olive oil
2 cloves garlic, peeled and crushed
6 peppercorns
1 teaspoon dried parsley
¼ teaspoon dried sweet basil
1 bay leaf
1 small onion, diced
¼ teaspoon salt
⅛ teaspoon dried oregano
¼ cup dried breadcrumbs
⅓ cup grated Parmesan cheese

1 Rinse gator steaks under running water. Pat dry and set aside.

2 Combine olive oil, garlic, peppercorns, parsley, basil, bay leaf, and onion in a shallow, covered dish or plastic bag with zipper seal. Add gator steaks to marinade and place in refrigerator. Marinate 3 to 4 hours, turning occasionally.

3 Blend breadcrumbs, salt, oregano and Parmesan cheese. Remove steaks from marinade and place in a shallow baking dish or casserole. Cover with breadcrumb mixture. Cover and bake at 350°F for 15 minutes. Uncover and bake for an additional 15 minutes or until gator meat reaches desired doneness.

Yield: 3 to 4 servings

Sweet and Sour Gator

2 pounds boneless alligator meat
3 green onions
1 large red pepper
3 tablespoons olive oil (divided)
½ teaspoon salt
1 20-ounce can pineapple chunks in juice
¼ cup granulated sugar
¼ cup cider vinegar
2 tablespoons catsup
1 teaspoon cornstarch
4 teaspoons low-sodium soy sauce

1 Rinse gator meat and pat dry with paper towel. Cut into bite-sized pieces. Cut onions into 1-inch pieces. Slice red pepper into ½-inch thick slices.

2 Heat 1 tablespoon olive oil in skillet over medium-high heat. Add green onions and red peppers and cook, stirring frequently, until tender but crisp. Remove vegetables with slotted spoon and drain on paper towels.

3 Add 2 tablespoons olive oil to same skillet and heat. Sprinkle gator meat with salt and cook in oil for 10 minutes or until done, stirring occasionally. Remove gator to plate.

4 Drain pineapple juice, reserving ¼ cup. In small bowl, mix reserved pineapple juice, sugar, vinegar, catsup, cornstarch and soy sauce.

5 Discard oil remaining in skillet. Return gator meat to skillet. Turn in pineapple mixture and heat to simmer. Cook until mixture thickens slightly. Stir in green onion/pepper mixture and pineapple chunks; heat thoroughly.

Yield: 5 servings

Campfire Wrapped Gator

If you're not the outdoor type, you may prepare this dish in a hot (425°F) oven using the same cooking time. Internal temperature of the thickest part of the gator steak should be 140°F. This recipe also works well with fish such as cod or haddock.

> 4 12-inch x 15-inch pieces of heavy-duty aluminum foil
> .4 alligator tail steaks, 8–10 ounces each
> ½ teaspoon dried oregano
> ½ teaspoon dried thyme
> ½ teaspoon paprika
> salt and pepper to taste
> 4 cloves garlic, peeled and minced
> 2 tablespoons butter or margarine
> 2 firm, ripe tomatoes, diced
> 2 teaspoons lemon juice
> 1 .large onion, sliced and separated into rings

1 Prepare campfire or charcoal grill and let it burn until logs or coals are hot and glowing. Cover cooking grill with foil and carefully place it over coals. If using a camp stove or a grill with a fuel source other than charcoal, pre-heat it to medium-high.

2 Place one gator steak crosswise in the center of each of the four pieces of aluminum foil. In a small mixing bowl, combine the oregano, thyme, paprika, salt and pepper. Sprinkle an equal amount of this herb mixture on both sides of each gator steak. Spread 1 minced clove of garlic over each steak. Dot each steak with ½ tablespoon of butter.

3 Combine tomatoes and lemon juice in a mixing bowl. Spoon ¼ of this mixture over each steak. Divide the onion ring slices evenly and arrange onion rings over each steak. Form a sealed foil packet around each steak by folding the long ends of the foil together first, then folding the sides together and turning the folds upward.

4 Using a long-handled heatproof spatula, place the packets in the center of your cooking surface. Cook for 15 to 20 minutes, depending on how hot the fire or grill is. Carefully remove each packet with the spatula and place it on a serving dish or other heatproof surface. Allow packets to cool for 5 minutes. Cautiously open each packet; using a spatula or long serving spoon, lift each gator steak and its toppings from the foil packet and place it on individual plate. Serve hot.

Yield: 4 servings

"HIS BELLY-RUB TO NAP RATIO IS LOWER THAN EVER... LOWELL'S TOO, FOR THAT MATTER."

Tangy Reptilian Ribs

½ cup molasses
¼ cup cider vinegar
¼ cup prepared yellow mustard
2 tablespoons Worcestershire sauce
½ teaspoon hot sauce
½ teaspoon salt
4 pounds alligator ribs

1 In a heavy saucepan, combine molasses, vinegar, mustard, Worcestershire sauce, hot sauce and salt. Bring mixture to a boil, remove from heat and set aside. Preheat oven to 450°F.

2 Cut ribs between every other rib bone, as they are small and delicate. Place the meatiest side down in a large baking dish. Bake covered for 15 minutes, then turn and bake an additional 15 minutes.

3 Brush ribs with sauce and cook 10 minutes. Turn ribs and brush with more sauce. Cook 10 minutes or until done.

Yield: 6 to 8 servings

GATOR FACT

How does an alligator wrestler put a gator "to sleep"? Flipping an alligator onto its back disrupts the blood flow to the area of its brain that controls vision, causing a sort of vertigo. The disoriented creature remains motionless until it is turned right-side-up again.

Kiwi and Key Lime Broiled Gator

Key limes are round and about the size of a golf ball. When ripe their color changes from green to yellow. If you aren't lucky enough to have Key limes, regular (Persian) lime juice and rind may be used.

4 medium kiwi fruit, peeled
2 tablespoons chopped red onion
4 teaspoons olive oil (divided)
3 teaspoons Key lime juice (divided)
½ teaspoon grated Key lime rind (divided)
¾ teaspoon salt (divided)
¼ teaspoon black ground pepper (divided)
¼ teaspoon paprika
vegetable oil cooking spray
4 alligator fillets, about 6 ounces each

1 Puree one kiwi fruit in blender or food processor. Place puree in bowl. Chop remaining kiwis and add to bowl. Add onion, 1 teaspoon oil, 1 teaspoon Key lime juice, ¼ teaspoon Key lime rind, ¼ teaspoon salt, and ⅛ teaspoon pepper. Stir and set aside.

2 Preheat broiler. Coat broiler pan with cooking spray.

3 Blend together remaining oil, Key lime juice and rind, paprika, salt, and pepper. Brush gator fillets with this mixture. Place gator on broiler pan rack.

4 Broil gator 3 minutes. Turn gator over and brush with lime mixture. Broil another 3 minutes or until gator is done.

5 Transfer to serving dish, pour kiwi sauce over gator and serve immediately.

Yield: 4 servings

Scrod-style Saurian

This recipe, suggested by 9-year-old Christopher, is traditionally made with cod.

4 alligator fillets, 6–8 ounces each
1 teaspoon salt
¼ teaspoon ground black pepper
¼ teaspoon onion powder
½ teaspoon paprika
¼ pound (1 stick) butter, melted
8 ounces Ritz or other buttery crackers
2 tablespoons grated Parmesan cheese
2 teaspoons fresh parsley, chopped

1 Preheat oven to 350°F. Rinse gator fillets and pat dry.

2 Sprinkle fillets with salt, pepper, onion powder, and paprika. Set aside.

3 Place crackers in plastic bag with zipper top. Crush with a rolling pin.

4 Melt butter in a small saucepan over medium heat. Remove pan from heat and toss in crushed crackers. Gently stir in Parmesan cheese and fresh parsley.

5 Place gator fillets in a shallow baking dish or casserole. Cover with cracker mixture and bake at 350°F for 30 to 40 minutes or until gator is thoroughly cooked.

Yield: 4 servings

Honey-grilled Gator Ribs

3–4 pounds alligator ribs
1 cup low-sodium soy sauce
1¼ teaspoons ground ginger
3 cloves garlic, peeled and crushed
⅔ cup brown sugar, firmly packed
1 cup honey
2 tablespoons butter or margarine
vegetable oil cooking spray

1 Rinse ribs and pat dry with paper towels. Cut ribs through to within ¾ inch and spread ribs. Place ribs in a shallow, covered dish or in a plastic bag with zipper top.

2 Combine soy sauce, ginger, and garlic; pour over ribs. Cover (or seal) and refrigerate for 4 hours. Turn ribs occasionally as they marinate.

3 Remove ribs from marinade. Discard marinade.

4 In a saucepan, combine brown sugar, honey, and butter. Cook over low heat, stirring constantly, until sugar dissolves.

5 Coat grill rack with cooking spray. Place rack 4 to 6 inches from heat source. Arrange ribs on grill; brush sauce on ribs and cook for 8 to 10 minutes on each side, or until juices run clear. Pour remaining sauce on ribs and serve.

Yield: 4 servings

Sizzling Saurian Sauerbraten

Planning ahead is a must when preparing this tasty dish, as the meat needs to marinate for 48 hours before cooking. Just as in the German recipe upon which this dish is based, it is an excellent method for preparing less-than-tender cuts of gator meat.

Marinade:
2 cups dry red wine
2 teaspoons salt
10 peppercorns, crushed
1 onion, thinly sliced
1 clove garlic, peeled and minced
2 teaspoons freshly ground ginger
1 bay leaf
2 tablespoons pickling spices
2 cups water

Sauerbraten:
1 4-pound alligator roast or tail section
3 tablespoons vegetable shortening
2 tablespoons butter
½ cup finely crushed gingersnap cookies
½ cup sour cream

1 Place gator meat in a deep glass casserole dish. In a saucepan, stir together the marinade ingredients and bring the mixture to a boil. Remove pan from heat and allow marinade to cool. Pour cooled marinade over alligator meat; cover the dish tightly and refrigerate for 48 hours, turning the meat in the marinade several a day.

2 Preheat oven to 350°F. Melt shortening and butter in a covered Dutch oven or heavy ovenproof skillet with lid. Remove gator meat from marinade and pat dry with paper towels. Sear gator meat in oil, turning to brown it on all sides.

3 Cover Dutch oven or skillet and bake for 2½ hours or until meat is done (meat thermometer in thickest part of roast should read 170°F).

4 Transfer meat to serving platter. Cut meat into thick slices. Place Dutch oven with pan drippings over low heat on stovetop. Add crushed gingersnaps to drippings and stir until the sauce is smooth and thick. Remove from heat and stir in sour cream. Pour sauce over sliced meat and serve.

Yield: 6 to 8 servings

GATOR FACT

Scientists have discovered that adult male alligators respond to the tone of B-flat by bellowing enthusiastically. This is the same note that alligators hit when they bellow—usually in the springtime, so as to impress any female gators who may be in the vicinity.

Coconut Crocodilian over Rice

This dish also works well with any firm, white fish.

2½ pounds firm alligator fillets
2 tablespoons lemon juice
¼ cup olive oil
1 medium onion, chopped
1 small red or yellow bell pepper, chopped
2 cloves garlic, peeled and crushed
3 plum tomatoes, diced
3 green onions, chopped, with tops
1 cup coconut milk
¼ teaspoon salt
1 bunch cilantro, finely chopped (optional)
2 tablespoons butter
¼ cup grated Parmesan cheese
4 cups cooked white rice
2 tablespoons shredded coconut

1 Wash gator fillets and pat dry with paper towels. Cut into bite-sized pieces, rub with lemon juice, and set aside. Heat olive oil in heavy skillet or Dutch oven. Add gator meat, onion, pepper and garlic. Cook over medium heat for 5 minutes or until onions are translucent. Add the tomatoes and green onions. Cover with coconut milk. Add salt and cilantro, if desired. Cover and simmer gently for about 8 minutes or until gator is done.

2 Add butter and Parmesan cheese to hot, cooked rice and stir until well mixed.

3 Arrange hot rice on platter. Spoon gator mixture over rice; sprinkle shredded coconut on top of gator and serve.

Yield: 4 servings

GOURMET GATOR DISHES

"... IT'S JUST THAT, FOR TODAY,
SEATING YOU TO MY LEFT SEEMED TO BE THE HIGHER QUALITY DECISION."

Alligator a L'Orange

This classic French dish is traditionally made with duck. Firm fish such as red snapper also works well with this recipe.

6 alligator fillets, 3–4 ounces each
vegetable oil cooking spray
3 tablespoons olive oil
2 tablespoons orange juice
3 tablespoons orange marmalade
¼ teaspoon salt
⅛ teaspoon ground white pepper
⅛ teaspoon ground nutmeg

1 Rinse gator fillets and pat dry. Preheat oven to 350°F. Spray baking dish with cooking spray. Arrange fillets in a single layer in baking dish and set aside.

2 Combine olive oil, marmalade, orange juice, salt, and pepper in a small bowl. Pour over the gator fillets.

3 Sprinkle fillets with nutmeg and bake 20 minutes or until gator is done.

Yield: 6 servings

BOWLING ALLEY GATOR
(ALLEYGUTTER)

Florida Gator Florentine

Veal or chicken fillets work well as substitutes for alligator in this recipe.

1 pound boneless alligator meat
4 peppercorns
1 10-ounce package frozen chopped spinach
2 tablespoons butter
½ teaspoon lemon juice
2 tablespoons all-purpose flour
2 cups milk
4 egg yolks, slightly beaten
¼ teaspoon salt
⅛ teaspoon ground black pepper
¼ teaspoon paprika
⅛ teaspoon ground nutmeg
1 small onion, minced
½ teaspoon minced parsley
2 hard-boiled eggs, chopped
¼ cup grated Parmesan cheese

1 Rinse gator meat and pat dry. Cut into bite-sized pieces. Heat 3 tablespoons of water in skillet. Add peppercorns and gator meat and cook, covered, for 5 minutes or until juices run clear. Remove gator with slotted spoon and set aside.

2 Cook spinach according to package directions, drain, and set aside.

3 Melt butter in saucepan. Gradually add flour, stirring constantly until smooth. Continuing to stir constantly, add milk. Cook until smooth and thick. Add egg yolks. Cook until just under boiling point; do not boil. Remove from heat and stir in the salt, pepper, paprika, nutmeg, onion, and parsley.

4 Preheat oven to 400°F. Butter a casserole dish. Spread the spinach evenly in the bottom of the casserole. Arrange gator meat on top of the spinach. Stir hard-cooked eggs into the sauce, then pour it over meat and spinach. Top with Parmesan cheese. Bake for 10 minutes.

Yield: 4 servings

Croc Au Vin

This dish, based on one created by family friend Mary Taylor, was inspired by the classic French peasant dish Coq Au Vin that is traditionally made with chicken. This recipe is an excellent choice for those less-than-tender cuts of meat.

Marinade:
2 cups Burgundy or other dry red wine
1 clove garlic, peeled and minced
6 whole cloves
6 whole peppercorns
6 coriander seeds
2 bay leaves
1 tablespoon dark brown sugar

Croc Au Vin:
2 pounds boneless alligator meat, cut into large, thick chunks
4 tablespoons olive oil
20 pearl onions
¼ pound center cut bacon, cut into ½-inch pieces
¼ cup brandy
2 cups Burgundy or other dry red wine (divided)
4 tablespoons all-purpose flour
1 teaspoon salt
1 clove garlic, peeled and minced
½ teaspoon dried thyme
12 small button mushrooms, sliced

1   Combine marinade ingredients in a shallow pan or casserole with a cover. Add alligator meat to this marinade. Cover and refrigerate for at least 2 hours (or overnight).

2   Heat oil in a heavy frying pan, preferably cast iron. Sauté onions in oil, stirring frequently, until they begin to brown. Add bacon to oil and onions and cook until bacon is done. Remove onions and bacon with a slotted spoon, drain on paper towels and set aside.

3 Remove gator meat from marinade and discard marinade. (Gator meat will have a reddish-purple tint.) Reheat oil in skillet and transfer gator meat to it; cook until meat is lightly brown. Remove skillet from heat. Sprinkle brandy over meat and ignite.

4 Add wine to skillet, reserving 2 tablespoons. Stir in the flour, then the salt, garlic, and thyme.

5 Toss mushrooms in 2 tablespoons of wine in a small bowl. Microwave on high for 2 minutes. Add mushrooms to skillet. Stir to blend all ingredients, cover and simmer for 10 minutes.

6 Add onions and bacon to gator meat in skillet. Stir to blend. Simmer 10 additional minutes or until gator meat is tender.

Yield: 4 servings

Alligator Fricassee

This dish is inspired by one traditionally prepared with poultry.

  2 teaspoons olive oil
  4 alligator fillets, 6 ounces each
  1 cup chopped sweet onion
  1 cup chopped celery
  1 cup chopped carrots (or parsnips)
  1 cup low-sodium chicken broth
  1 cup water
  ½ cup brown rice
  2 teaspoons ground paprika
  salt to taste
  ½ teaspoon ground white pepper
  1 cup frozen peas, thawed
  4 medium-sized plum tomatoes, cut into quarters

1 In a Dutch oven or large, heavy skillet, heat olive oil; add gator and cook for 5 minutes, turning pieces to brown both sides. Remove fillets and set aside.

2 Add onions, celery and carrots (or parsnips) to pan; cook and stir for 5 minutes or until tender. Return fillets to skillet. Add chicken broth and water; bring to a boil.

3 Stir in rice, paprika, salt, and pepper. Reduce heat to low; cover and simmer for 45 minutes, until rice is tender and liquid is absorbed.

4 Stir in peas and tomatoes and cook for an additional two minutes or until heated through.

Yield: 4 servings

Croc Cordon Bleu

4 tablespoons butter or margarine, melted
½ cup fresh or packaged breadcrumbs
¾ teaspoon salt
¼ teaspoon paprika
8 alligator fillets, about 3 ounces each
4 thin slices of cooked ham, each about 3 inches square
4 1-ounce pieces of Gruyere cheese, each about 2 inches square

1 Preheat oven to 400°F. Coat bottom and sides of baking dish with butter, margarine or vegetable oil cooking spray. Place remaining melted butter in shallow dish; set aside.

2 Mix breadcrumbs with salt and paprika.

3 Dip each fillet in melted butter. Place ham and cheese between two fillets. Secure the two fillets with wooden toothpicks.

4 Brush tops and bottoms of fillet packets with more butter, if needed, and roll fillets in breadcrumb mixture until well coated.

5 Place fillet packets in buttered baking dish and bake for 35 minutes or until brown. (The thicker your fillets, the longer this dish will take to cook. If the fillets are less than one inch thick, reduce the cooking time accordingly.)

Yield: 4 servings

GATOR FACT

An adult alligator has 82 sharp, hollow, replaceable teeth. When one tooth falls out, a new one grows in. Over the course of its lifetime, an alligator may go through as many as 3,000 teeth.

Super Saurian Stroganoff

Although traditionally made with beef, a good stroganoff may also be made with seafood. Shrimp, lobster tail, or a combination of the two are delicious alternative ingredients for this recipe.

> 1 pound boneless alligator meat
> 1 tablespoon olive oil
> ½ pound fresh mushrooms, sliced
> 1 medium sweet onion, chopped
> 1 green bell pepper, chopped
> 2 cloves garlic, peeled and chopped
> ¼ cup butter
> ½ cup all-purpose flour
> ⅔ cup water
> ½ teaspoon salt
> ½ teaspoon ground black pepper
> 8 ounces sour cream
> 4 cups cooked wide egg noodles
> 2 tablespoons fresh chives, chopped

1 Rinse gator meat and pat dry with paper towels. Thinly slice gator meat into 1-inch by 3-inch strips. Set aside.

2 Heat olive oil in large, heavy skillet or Dutch oven. Add gator meat, mushrooms, onion, pepper and garlic. Sauté, turning frequently, for 5 minutes, or until meat is lightly browned and onions are soft. Remove items from skillet with a slotted spoon and drain on a paper towel. Set aside.

3 Melt butter in skillet or Dutch oven over low heat Add flour an stir until smooth. Cook for 1 minute, stirring constantly and gradually adding water. Return sautéed vegetables and gator to skillet or Dutch oven. Add salt and pepper. Cover and simmer for 30 minutes. Remove from heat and gently stir in sour cream. Heat thoroughly.

4 Spoon gator mixture over cooked noodles. Garnish with chopped chives and serve hot.

Yield: 4 servings

Prehistoric Primavera

In Spanish, primavera means "spring". This dish can be made with your favorite springtime vegetables in place of the ones suggested.

¾ pound boneless alligator meat
2 tablespoons olive oil
3 peppercorns
1 sweet onion, chopped
1 red bell pepper, chopped
3 cloves garlic, peeled and minced
½ cup fresh mushrooms, sliced
½ cup broccoli florets, fresh or frozen
¼ cup water
1½ cups milk or half-and-half
½ cup grated Parmesan cheese
2 tablespoons butter
1 teaspoon dried basil
½ teaspoon salt
¼ teaspoon ground black pepper
2 cups cooked long grain rice

1 Rinse gator meat and pat dry. Cut into bite-sized pieces.

2 Heat olive oil over medium-high heat in heavy skillet or Dutch oven. Place gator meat in skillet with peppercorns. Cook for 2 minutes, stirring constantly. Add onions, pepper, and garlic and cook an additional 3 minutes, continuing to stir. Add mushrooms and broccoli and cook, stirring, for 3 minutes longer. Add water and bring mixture to a boil.

3 Reduce heat to simmer. Stir in milk or cream, Parmesan cheese, butter, basil, salt, and pepper. Add cooked rice and heat thoroughly. Remove from heat, cover, and let stand for 5 minutes. Fluff with a fork and serve.

Yield: 4 servings

Luscious Alligator Louis

vegetable oil cooking spray
1 pound alligator fillet
¼ teaspoon salt
¼ teaspoon paprika
1 clove garlic, peeled and crushed
2 tablespoons water
4 peppercorns
¾ cup mayonnaise
¼ cup chili sauce
2 tablespoons minced parsley
2 tablespoons white vinegar
½ teaspoon Worcestershire sauce
¼ teaspoon prepared horseradish
8 large Romaine lettuce leaves, rinsed and thoroughly dried

1 Spray skillet with cooking spray. Cut gator meat into bite-sized pieces and sprinkle it with salt and paprika. Heat skillet over medium-high heat. Place gator bits and garlic in skillet and cook for 2 minutes, turning frequently, until lightly browned. Add water and peppercorns. Cook for an additional 5 to 6 minutes or until gator is done. Remove gator with a slotted spoon and drain on paper towels.

2 In a mixing bowl, combine mayonnaise, chili sauce, parsley, vinegar, Worcestershire sauce, and horseradish. Mix well. Add gator meat and toss to coat. Cover and refrigerate 2 or more hours until chilled throughout.

3 Arrange lettuce on a serving plate and top with gator mixture.

Yield: 4 servings

Find
the
Gator

Curried Gator Afrikaans

1 medium-sized tart green apple
1½ pounds boneless alligator meat
1 tablespoon olive oil
¼ cup butter
1 small sweet onion, chopped
2 cloves garlic, peeled and chopped
1 medium-sized ripe banana
¼ cup all-purpose flour
1 cup milk
1 cup light cream
1 tablespoon curry powder
½ teaspoon paprika
¼ teaspoon salt
6 cups cooked rice
2 tablespoons chopped fresh chives

1 Peel and core apple. Cut into small chunks.

2 Rinse gator meat and pat dry with paper towels. Cut into 2-inch by 3-inch chunks. Heat olive oil and butter over medium heat. Add gator chunks and sauté for 3 to 5 minutes; add onion, garlic, apple, and banana. Stirring frequently, cook an additional 5 minutes until gator juices run clear and onion is soft but not brown.

3 Reduce heat to low. Stirring constantly, add flour and then milk and cream.

4 Continue constant stirring as you add the curry powder, paprika, and salt. Cook until the sauce is thick and bubbly. Spoon over cooked rice, garnish with fresh chives, and serve.

Yield: 6 servings

Alligator Bisque

6 cups fish stock or low-sodium chicken broth
1½ pounds boneless alligator meat
5 peppercorns
1 small onion, sliced
2 stalks celery, sliced
1 carrot, sliced
2 cloves garlic, peeled and minced
1 bay leaf
3 sprigs parsley, chopped
1 teaspoon salt
¼ teaspoon ground black pepper
¼ teaspoon ground nutmeg
¼ teaspoon paprika
5 tablespoons butter
2½ tablespoons all-purpose flour
1 cup light cream

1 In stockpot, heat 1 cup of broth over medium-high heat. Cut gator meat into bite-sized pieces. Put gator and peppercorns in pot and cook for 5 minutes.

2 Add onions, celery, carrot, garlic, bay leaf, parsley, salt, pepper, nutmeg, and paprika. Reduce heat, cover, and simmer for 30 minutes, stirring occasionally. Remove from heat and strain, reserving stock. Set meat and vegetables mixture aside and return stock to pot.

3 Melt 3 tablespoons butter in saucepan. Add flour and stir until smooth. Simmer for 1 minute. Add flour mixture to stock and blend. Bring stock to a boil, stirring constantly. Reduce heat and simmer 4 minutes.

4 Remove bay leaf and add meat and vegetables to stock. Slowly stir in cream. Mix well and simmer until heated thoroughly. Sprinkle with paprika and serve.

Yield: 6 servings

Gator Creole

1½ pounds boneless alligator meat
6 tablespoons butter
1 large sweet onion, chopped
6 stalks of celery, chopped
1 medium-sized green bell pepper, cut into ½-inch strips
1 medium-sized red bell pepper, cut into ½-inch strips
4 cloves garlic, peeled and minced
6 large firm, ripe tomatoes, peeled
2 teaspoons dried basil
2 teaspoons dried thyme
6–8 drops hot sauce
1 tablespoon lemon juice
1 teaspoon salt
½ teaspoon ground black pepper
2 tablespoons fresh parsley, chopped

1 Rinse and dry gator meat. Cut into bite-sized pieces and set aside.

2 Melt butter in heavy saucepan or Dutch oven over medium heat. Place gator meat in skillet and cook for 3 minutes. Add onions and cook until transparent. Add celery, peppers and garlic. Sauté, stirring frequently for an additional 3 minutes.

3 Add tomatoes, basil, thyme, hot sauce, lemon juice, salt, and pepper. Cover and cook for 10 minutes or until meat is done.

4 Garnish with fresh parsley and serve.

Yield: 4 servings

Golden Gator Scampi-style

Scampi is a crustacean found in the Adriatic Sea. Since it is seldom available in the U.S., this dish is usually made with large shrimp.

1½ pounds boneless alligator meat
¼ pound butter
1 small onion, finely minced
4 cloves garlic, peeled and finely minced
1 2-ounce jar sliced mushrooms
½ teaspoon salt
¼ teaspoon ground black pepper
½ teaspoon paprika
1 tablespoon parsley, chopped

1 Rinse gator meat and cut into bite-sized pieces.

2 Melt butter in heavy skillet over medium-high heat. Place gator meat in skillet and sauté for 5 minutes, turning frequently. Add onion, garlic and mushrooms to skillet and cook an additional 5 minutes or until meat is browned and onions are soft.

3 Place meat and sautéed vegetables on serving plate and pour butter mixture over meat. Sprinkle with salt, pepper and paprika. Garnish with parsley and serve.

Yield: 4 servings

GATOR FACT
Alligators reach ages of 35–40 years in the wild, 50–60 years in captivity. Typically, females have much shorter life spans than males.

Tandoori Gator

Pre-mixed Tandoori spices can be substituted in this marinade, which is also good used with thin fish such as flounder, and with chicken. Remember to adjust cooking times if you choose a different meat or thicker fillets.

Marinade:
1 cup plain yogurt
¼ teaspoon salt
⅛ teaspoon ground black pepper
1 clove garlic, peeled and crushed
½ teaspoon grated ginger
1 teaspoon paprika
1 teaspoon ground cumin
1 teaspoon ground coriander
1 pound ½-inch-thick alligator fillets
vegetable oil cooking spray

1 Combine all marinade ingredients in a shallow bowl and mix well. Add the gator fillets and turn to coat them with marinade, Cover and refrigerate 3 to 4 hours, turning fillets from time to time to keep them coated with marinade.

2 Spray broiler pan with cooking spray. Preheat broiler. Remove fillets from marinade and place on broiler pan in a single layer. Broil fillets on one side for 3 to 4 minutes. Turn fillets and broil for an additional 3 to 4 minutes or until meat is cooked thoroughly.

Yield: 4 servings

Gator Tail Marsala

The white tail meat of the alligator is most similar in texture and flavor to veal. That makes it an excellent choice for this dish, which is traditionally made with veal.

12 ounces alligator tail cutlets
4 tablespoons all-purpose flour
1 tablespoon olive oil (divided)
⅔ cup Marsala wine
2 cloves garlic, peeled and minced
1 cup fresh mushrooms, sliced
1 sweet onion, sliced and separated into rings
1 red bell pepper, sliced into ¼-inch strips
1½ cups low-sodium chicken broth
2 teaspoons lemon juice
¼ teaspoon dried basil
½ teaspoon salt
½ teaspoon ground black pepper
2 cups fettuccine noodles, cooked per package directions
2 tablespoons chopped fresh parsley

1 Place each gator tail cutlet between two sheets of wax paper or plastic wrap and pound it with a meat mallet or rolling pin until it is ¼ inch thick. Cut meat into 2-inch squares. Dredge in flour.

2 Heat 1½ teaspoons olive oil in a heavy skillet over medium heat. Add gator cutlets and cook 2 to 3 minutes on each side until brown. Transfer meat to a lightly greased casserole. Pour wine into skillet and deglaze by stirring to loosen drippings. Pour skillet contents over gator. Preheat oven to 400°F.

3 Heat remaining olive oil in skillet. Combine garlic, mushrooms, onion, and bell pepper in skillet and cook for 2 minutes. Add broth, lemon juice, basil, salt and pepper. Cook until vegetables are tender. Pour over gator meat. Bake for 15 minutes. Serve over fettuccine noodles. Garnish with parsley.

Yield: 4 servings

Perfect Paella with Alligator

Paella is a traditional dish of Spain. The bright yellow color that the saffron gives to the rice makes this a festive dish. While rice, olive oil and saffron are the primary ingredients, a variety of seafood can be used and a paella may also include chicken.

¼ cup olive oil
1½ pounds boneless alligator meat
¼ pound garlic sausage, thinly sliced
12 medium-sized raw shrimp
1 onion, finely chopped
2 cloves garlic, peeled and minced
1 red bell pepper, cut into thin, ½ inch-long strips
1¾ cups long grain rice*
½ teaspoon paprika
⅛ teaspoon powdered saffron
3½ cups fish stock or low-sodium chicken broth
1 cup frozen green peas, thawed
12 fresh mussels, cleaned (or 8-ounce can mussels, drained)
4 plum tomatoes, skinned, seeded and chopped
½ teaspoon salt
¼ teaspoon ground black pepper
¼ teaspoon dried oregano
2 tablespoons fresh parsley, chopped

1 Heat oil in Dutch oven or heavy skillet. Cut gator meat into 2-inch pieces. Add gator meat and garlic sausage to oil and cook for 5 minutes or until browned. Remove meat with slotted spoon, setting it aside on paper towels to drain.

2 Shell shrimp; make a slit down the back of shrimp and remove the black sand vein. Set aside.

3 Add onion, garlic and red pepper to skillet and cook until onions are tender. Stir in rice and mix well. Add the paprika, saffron and fish stock or broth. Bring mixture to a boil. Reduce heat and simmer for 15 minutes.

4 Stir in gator meat, sausage, peas, shelled shrimp, mussels, tomatoes, salt, and pepper. Simmer an additional 10 to 15 minutes until peas and gator are thoroughly heated and shrimp are pink.

Yield: 6 servings

✱ In some southern states, prepared yellow rice mixes that already include the saffron are available. If you are using one of those mixes in place of the rice, eliminate the saffron, paprika, salt, and pepper.

" I DON'T KNOW . . . HE REALLY LIKES
SITTING UP FRONT BY THE WINDOW, SO . . . I LET HIM."

Country Croc Cassoulet

Hearty French stews of meat and beans called cassoulets ("cass-o-LAYS") were the inspiration for this dish. Often they are made from veal or lamb, but any red meat works well.

    2   tablespoons olive or canola oil
    2   small sweet onions, sliced into rings
    2   cloves of garlic, minced
    2   green bell peppers, seeded and diced
    ⅛   teaspoon ground cloves
    1   pound ground alligator meat (see note page 32)
    1   pound alligator sausage, cut into ¼-inch slices
    3   medium carrots, thinly sliced
    ½   cup chopped celery
    1   16-ounce can kidney beans, drained
    1   16-ounce can great northern beans, drained
    1   14½-ounce can black beans, drained
    1   15-ounce can Italian-style tomato sauce
    6   plum tomatoes, diced
    ½   cup dark corn syrup
    ½   cup red wine
    1   teaspoon dry mustard
    1   teaspoon dried oregano
    1   teaspoon dried thyme
    2   teaspoons salt
    ½   teaspoon ground black pepper

1 Preheat oven to 375°F. Heat oil in heavy skillet or Dutch oven over medium high heat. Place onions, garlic, green pepper and ground cloves in oil. Stir and cook 2 minutes or until onions are soft and slightly brown. Add ground gator meat and gator sausage. Cook, stirring frequently, until meat is crumbly and brown and sausage is browned on all sides. Remove from heat.

2 Combine all remaining ingredients in a large mixing bowl and stir to mix well. Add to meat mixture in skillet, tossing to mix. If mixture appears too thick, stir in ¼ to ½ cup water.

3 Cover and bake for 60 minutes or until carrots and celery are tender.

Yield: 8 to 10 servings

Reptile Ratatouille

1 pound alligator fillets
2 cups water
1 zucchini, peeled and cubed
1 yellow summer squash, peeled and cubed
1 eggplant, peeled and cubed
4 tablespoons olive oil
1 sweet onion, peeled and chopped
2 cloves garlic, peeled and crushed
1 28-ounce can diced tomatoes, drained
1 teaspoon dried oregano
1 teaspoon dried parsley
½ teaspoon paprika
1 bay leaf
½ teaspoon salt
¼ teaspoon ground black pepper
4 ounces sliced mozzarella cheese
4 ounces sliced Swiss cheese
2 tablespoons grated Parmesan cheese

1 Rinse gator fillets under running water. Pat dry with paper towel. Thinly slice gator meat into 1-inch by 3-inch strips and set aside.

2 Bring water to a boil in saucepan. Add zucchini, squash and eggplant to boiling water and cook for 10 minutes. Drain vegetables and set aside.

3 Heat olive oil in a skillet over medium heat. Add onion, garlic and gator meat to skillet and sauté, stirring frequently, for 7 to 8 minutes or until gator meat is browned and onion is tender. Add cooked vegetable mixture, tomatoes, oregano, parsley, paprika, bay leaf, salt and pepper. Reduce heat to low and simmer, uncovered, for 20 minutes.

4 Coarsely grate mozzarella and Swiss cheeses together in a mixing bowl. Add grated Parmesan cheese and stir to mix well. Set aside.

5 Transfer gator and vegetable mixture to an ungreased shallow baking pan or casserole. Sprinkle cheese mixture evenly on top of gator mixture and place under broiler until cheese is hot and bubbly.

Yield: 6 servings

Greek Gator Pilaf

1 medium onion, finely chopped
2 tablespoons butter
2 tablespoons olive oil
1 alligator fillet, about 8 ounces
1½ cups water
1 cup uncooked brown rice
½ teaspoon dried oregano
⅛ teaspoon garlic powder
¼ teaspoon salt
⅛ teaspoon ground black pepper
2 plum tomatoes, each cut into eight chunks

1 Heat butter and olive oil in a heavy skillet or Dutch oven over medium heat. Add onion and sauté until golden brown.

2 Cut gator into bite-sized pieces. Brown gator in butter and olive oil, turning frequently until brown, about 5 minutes.

3 Add water, rice, oregano, garlic, salt, pepper, and tomatoes. Cover, reduce heat, and simmer for 25 minutes.

Yield: 6 servings

Cartoon by Christopher Dale Stevens